Soup and Bread

Soup and Bread

100 RECIPES for BOWL & BOARD

Julia Older and Steve Sherman

with a foreword by M.F.K. Fisher

Drawings by Jim Arnosky

• THE STEPHEN GREENE PRESS •

Brattleboro, Vermont

This book has been produced
in the United States of America.
It is designed by R. L. Dothard Associates
and published by The Stephen Greene Press,
Brattleboro, Vermont 05301

LIBRARY OF CONGRESS CATALOGING IN PUBLICATION DATA

Older, Julia, 1941–
  Soup and bread.

  Includes index.
  1. Soups. 2. Bread. I. Sherman, Steve, 1938–
joint author. II. Title.
TX757.043   641.8'13   78-14282
ISBN 0-8289-0336-0

PUBLISHED DECEMBER 1978
Second printing August 1979
Third printing May 1980

Contents

A Foreword

by M.F.K. Fisher

It is impossible to think of any good meal, no matter how plain or elegant, without soup or bread in it. It is almost as hard to find any recorded menu, ancient or modern, without one or both . . . just as it is to read a book, or walk through a museum, without savoring one or both on the page, the canvas . . . the mind's palate.

Of course bread and soup, being thus intrinsic to our survival, can be deeply personal things to the fortunate among us who are blessed with fearless memory. We read, for instance, about a soup served to an Egyptian princess or a Roman tyrant, or about bread broken long ago in the country called Israel—and then we taste, according to our cultural empathy and our gastronomical curiosity. But what we savor more keenly than these, if we are both lucky and honest, is a dusty soda cracker stolen from the pocket of a fat schoolfriend (shamed delight), or two bowls of a rich vegetable broth drunk lickety-split after a childhood fever (voluptuous satiety).

I have always been fortunate in this trick of recalling past pleasures, especially in times of inner drought and stress. They are food for the spirit. This is one reason why it is satisfying to find an intelligently compiled, sensitive, practical book called, with a simplicity that is reassuring, *Soup and Bread*.

It is evocative, as all good things should be . . . on the page, the plate, the mind. It is well put together, so that a soup, and a good bread to go with it or even to follow it, face each other on the pages. Nobody need agree with how the authors have paired their recipes, for they can be used in any personal jumble. I myself would not like a Sally Lunn with

Artichoke Soup; that is, my mental taste buds say that I would not. But I must think more about it . . . try it. . . .

The book evokes enjoyments, sensual memories. There is a good recipe for *Pan Dulce,* for instance, and reading, once more I am in the early market in a Mexican village, buying a warm sweet roll from a woman who walked for hours down the hills with the night's baking in a coarse cloth on her head. The bread was spicy, surprisingly rich for that spare country. I ate it from a piece of oily newspaper on the counter of a little open-front bar, and drank a local beer with it instead of the thick *sopa* suggested in this book, and it was a long time ago, but the taste of coriander and dark sugar and fresh-baked dough is still fresh.

It seems strange to me by now that when I was a child we were rescued by Sustaining Broths when we had been ill, and that the only real soup I remember eating with my parents was a rare Oyster Stew on the Sunday nights when Grand-mother, our gastronomic mentor, was away. Of course, when I was drinking the invalid broths and downing the memorable Oyster Stews of my early days, the question of finding good bread was not yet dreamed of. Bread was good, that's all. The flour was good, and so was the water. If the current cook did not have a light hand with the dough, there was an excellent baker in town. Toast for breakfast, treats after school with strawberry jam, dried crusts for Bread Pudding stiff with raisins: we never *doubted.* We thrived.

Our gamut of baked breads was as limited as were our soups, almost: white, Graham, now and then hot baking pow-der biscuits or corn bread. The last two were 'special' and served only at noon, but the others were ubiquitous. They were *there,* supposedly our right and privilege.

Once a very old woman told me what her even older grandmother had told her about Bread Soup. Across about a hundred and fifty years I heard again of the most comforting thing that could be eaten on this earth, at least in the days when the makings were unpolluted: broken pieces from yes-terday's loaf, in a bowl, with a ladleful of boiling water poured over it and, on a feastday, a sprinkle of salt. This, the old, old woman told me through generations of gradually corrupted palates, was the best food in the world to comfort and bring sweet sleep.

Such a recipe is not found in a collection like this one. Indeed, its austerity is almost impossible to evoke with the mind's palate, so long has it been for us since a child in about 1830 could find celestial what we would call prison punishment. Today's bread, today's water, even the iodinized fluoridated salt? No.

That is another reason why this book is worth pondering. It nourishes us with simplicity, adjusted to our times, but also with many subtleties that are as amusing as they are plain. Why not put canned apricot juice in Cock-a-leekie Soup? It is logical, if you can read. And why not serve beer with one soup, milk with another, a Zinfandel here and a sparkling wine there? And the suggestion that sweet butter and wild grape jelly would do well with popovers! It is so sensuous that the scalp prickles . . . centuries from a child's dream of bread-and-water. . . .

We can be helped, in this less innocent world, to reach back a little in a book like *Soup and Bread*. Why not make something like Vegetable-Short Rib Soup, and some Wheat Germ Crackers . . . find some good cold milk . . . help a child of this century rise again?

Preface

It is fatuous for a cookbook to claim that all its recipes originated in the author's kitchen. Cooking is integral to civilization and civilization has been cooking soups and breads for millennia.

What we *can* say is that all the recipes included here were tested specifically for this book. Nearly all have been in our personal collection of favorites; some we ran across recently. The recipes come from friends and relatives, very old cookbooks and new ones alike. A few we've created completely from scratch, most we modified to fit our own tastes.

We tried to select and pair the soups and breads judiciously. The bread on the right-hand side of the open page accompanies the soup on the left-hand side. Together with the subjoined beverage, fruit, cheese or salad suggested to go with them, any pair makes a complete meal, either a light lunch, as the cold minted pea soup and honey lime rolls, or a full dinner, as the duck soup and orange almond loaf. Of course, the soups and breads may be paired other ways at your own preference.

The axiom goes that if a cookbook has at least one good recipe you can't resist, it's a success. We hope you find that one and many more in *Soup and Bread*.

J.O.
S.S.

Soup

Pease Porridge Hot, Pease Porridge Cold,
Pease Porridge in the Pot Nine Days Old

THE WORD SOUP is related to the word *supper*, an evening meal of liquid food. Yet all the words in the world can't substitute for actually smelling the rich herb-scented aroma of a simmering soup and then tasting the vibrancy of a well-balanced creation that leads you helplessly from one spoonful to the next.

Soups are as ancient as cooking and as close as your kitchen. In fact, making soups lets you participate in the long stream of history and tradition. Colonial fireplaces were built with a swinging iron hook that suspended the soup cauldron over the fire. When wood stoves replaced fireplace cookery, the soup pot was still a standard fixture on the back burner. Early gas and electric stoves were made with deep wells which substituted for the traditional soup pot. One of the first stoves I cooked on had a deep well—the feature that started me making soup. The well kept the temperature uniform so that I could cover it, leave for work, and be assured of a one-pot supper upon my return. Today the crockpot has usurped this role in many kitchens. Some of the recipes here may be made in your crockpot, but the more delicate milk- or cream-based bisques and chowders require sauce pans, which are more convenient for stirring.

For the broth-based soups that demand initial sautéing or braising, I find that a large iron frying pan or Dutch oven works well. These are also handy for any soup that is placed in the oven. Most good soup chefs use huge copper kettles, but these are very expensive. Copper-bottomed stainless steel or heavy enamel kettles will do. (Aluminum is to be avoided: it doesn't conduct heat as evenly as copper or steel, and it may introduce toxins in food that can build up in the body.)

Stock

Most soups are based on some sort of stock or broth. Beef, chicken, veal, fish, vegetables, or a combination of these ingredients, are boiled in water until the liquid is saturated with their essence. This is stock. It isn't at all difficult to make, and yet many cooks build their soups on store-bought stocks. These commercial "soup starters" are filled with additives, are oversalted, and usually don't taste anywhere near your own back burner pot boiler.

Making your own stock saves you money in the long run, because not only do you eat the stock, but also the beef or chicken that made it. The chicken that produced a rich golden stock one day may in turn be used in a chicken salad sandwich or a chicken pot pie the next.

Any stock not used in the soup may be stored a few days in the refrigerator, or poured into a freezer container or ice cube tray and frozen for future use.

There's a Garden in My Soup

Some people are of the opinion that taking all your leftovers from the refrigerator and adding a few cans of chicken noodle makes an excellent soup. I'm not one of them. The recipes in this book are designed for the freshest choice ingredients available. Garden-fresh vegetables and herbs make the best soups.

Herbs and spices are essential to most of the following soups. Some spices, such as curry powder, are difficult to make in the home and must be bought. Others, such as parsley and basil, may be grown in pots all year around.

In order to achieve the full aroma and essence of the herb in the soup, it must either be cooked a long time in the liquid or be sautéed first in butter or oil. A *bouquet garni* is usually indicated when the herbs must be removed from the soup in order to purée it or make a liaison.

Just as your herbs should be fresh, soup wines should be of good quality. An inferior wine will produce an inferior soup.

Salt and Pepper

Perhaps the most injurious insult to a cook is to watch a guest indiscriminately salt and pepper food before taking one bite. Through overuse salt has nearly lost its savor in this country. As a test, try eating sweet butter a week or two and then go back to salted butter. It will be distastefully salty.

On purpose I have avoided measurements for salt and pepper in our recipes. The cook must use his or her own discretion. Most meats, cheeses, and vegetables have a natural sodium content. These must cook first to release the natural salts before table salt is added.

Pepper varies in taste: white, black and red pepper—each is distinctive. White pepper and peppercorns are usually indicated for light broths and cream soups in which black pepper would not be visually appealing. Freshly ground black pepper tastes more lively, and cayenne is the hottest of the three.

Food Mill, Blender, or Food Processor?

Which to use, and when? The food mill has one advantage that neither the blender nor the food processor have. In milling the food through a fine disc, the tougher fibers found in some foods are extracted (blenders and processors only chop them up). This is the reason a food mill is recommended in Artichoke Soup. When a purée is called for, any one of the three may be used. The food processor is especially helpful when large quantities of vegetables must be chopped or diced as in Meat Borscht.

You Can Judge a Soup by Its Bowl

A clear amber consommé will not reach its visual potential served in a peasant-style pottery bowl. Nor will a Bohemian borscht lend itself to a dainty Limoges cup. Try to select the appropriate dish to fit the character of your soup:

ovenproof gratin dishes
standard soup bowls
shallow soup plates
deep pottery or earthenware bowls
pottery mugs
Oriental rice bowls
China tea cups

wine or water goblets
glass compotes
punch cups and saucers
marmites (individual casseroles)
double-handled soup cups
serving tureens

Garnish

Garnish means "to ornament with something bright and savory," nothing more, nothing less. The garnish should never upstage the soup itself. Those included with the soup recipes are just suggestions. Many others may be substituted, from

French fried parsley to slivered almonds. The end of your imagination is the end of the list.

The Versatile Soup

Some soups aren't fussy. They take a soupçon of this or that. If you err and put in more this than that, the soup will survive. Others, such as clarified consommé and white onion wine soup, require closer attention. The novice soup maker will be able to tell from the list of ingredients just how carefully to follow the recipe.

If, for example, the soup calls for eight cups of liquid and coarsely chopped vegetables to be cooked for three hours, not much emphasis need be applied to exacting detail. A soup of this nature would be a good jumping off point for the inexperienced souperman or woman.

The soups in this book are piping hot or ice-cold; mild or spicy; thick or thin; transparent or opaque; white, yellow, green, red, orange, brown, black. Some may be eaten as a light lunch or appetizer, and others as a one-pot meal. Some are completely vegetable; others meat and vegetable. A few are exotic (artichoke soup), a few, old standards (tomato soup). One or two take on strange wonderful forms (molded Chinese soup) and one is even dry (dry soup or sopa seca).

Soup, ever versatile.

J.O.

Bread

LIFE WITHOUT BREAD is unthinkable. French toast for
breakfast, sandwiches for lunch, rolls for dinner—on
and on with endless variations bread permeates our
daily lives. It gives us more pleasure, food energy, and satisfaction than most of us realize, and yet we take it too much
for granted, like the air we breathe and the good Earth we
walk on.

Bread is central to every ordinary day. Then why have
bread without life? Why always eat the same kind of loaf with
the same shape and same seasoning? Why, when it's so easy to
try something fresh and new?

Bread Is Easy

Baking bread is a snap. A lot of verbiage has been written
about the therapeutic, culinary, and Zen exotics of breadmaking, giving the impression that if you slip and use a teaspoon
of oil instead of a tablespoon all your kneading and mixing
and waiting will end in abject failure. Your loaf will hate you.

On the contrary. Your loaf is a friendly sort. It's totally on
your side, with tolerances that are extremely generous. The
recipes here are scripts to be interpreted, not regulations to
be glued to. They're all easy. Because if something goes
wrong, it's easy to try again. I learned this in a Lilliputian

log-cabin village in Alaska where I lived for a time. The town was on the edge of the Yukon River in the remote bush country. You made your bread or you ate no bread.

Breadmaking is simply getting in there and doing it. No Mongolian emperor is going to lop off your head because you killed the yeast. Just plunge ahead. Mix some salt into the flour. Add some yeast. Pour in some water. Stir it around. Knead it and beat it around. Let the yeast work for you an hour or two. Round up the dough into a loaf shape. Stick it in a pan, shove it in the oven. And there it is—golden, crusty smelly, high, wide, and irresistible.

Electric bread mixers aren't mentioned in the following recipes. Instead of beating a thin batter 200 strokes or so with a wooden spoon, as suggested, you may wish to use an electric mixer for two or three minutes. You may even elect to use a bread mixer for the kneading. If you do, you'll subtract some of the effort, but you'll also subtract some of the satisfaction. The pleasure of baking bread is in your *own* mixing, beating, and kneading of the dough; this is important to the full enjoyment of the end result. It's the close sensual feel of turning flour into loaves that you don't want to miss.

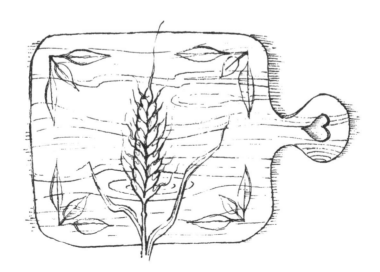

For the last fifteen years I've bought at most a dozen loaves of commercial bread. Why should I? Homemade bread far surpasses storebought bread in taste, freshness, quality of ingredients, and cost, not to mention in giving you the pleasure of making something that didn't exist before, sculpturing your own food, knowing exactly what goes into your loaf, and sniffing the sumptuous bread-baking aroma from the oven, as has been done throughout human history.

Ingredients

The bread recipes in this book have a pattern to them. The basic loaves have little or no sweetening. Those that do use honey, not sugar, when feasible, since honey imparts a deeper crust, lightly golden interior, longer storage time, and adds a few trace elements for nutrition. No margarine, which is highly chemical, is used. Only sweet, unsalted butter is suggested to give a mellower, better tasting bread.

Also, corn oil is used to lubricate bread pans and baking sheets. Oil tastes better than vegetable shortening, gives a crustier exterior, and has no array of hydrogenating preservatives, as do most (not all) shortenings. Unbleached flour is used for white flour, and minimal amounts of salt are suggested. When feasible, lively yeast takes precedence over inorganic baking powder.

Ordinary dry yeast purchased in supermarkets has never failed me. I buy it in two-pound cans at great savings, measure it out by the tablespoon, and store it in glass jars. Using wet yeast cakes is an anachronistic waste of time and effort.

These are indeed merely suggestions, but I've found that they work well in both preparation and taste.

Directions

On the whole, the recipes in this book are designed for smaller yields, serving four and six people to coincide with the soups. Generally, a second rising of the bread dough is eliminated, mostly to reduce time. A lighter textured bread does result from a second major rising, but one rising before shaping and the final rising works well.

The oven may also cut down some rising time. Frequently, I turn on the oven to 200 degrees or less, turn it off, and place the covered dough inside. The easy heat speeds up the yeast action but does not cook the dough. Pay attention if you do this for final rising. If the temperature is too hot, the dough will rise too fast unevenly.

Whatever the method you prefer or develop, baking your own bread will by its very nature bring you closer to some of the essences of life itself. Some breads, in fact, can be baked to include all necessary nutrients to sustain you indefinitely. Soy bread in this book is one. And yet as nutrition-conscious as the public is becoming, the plain fact is that taste has, does, and always will take precedence over health in our enjoyment of food. When the two are combined, however—as they are in good bread—then the pleasure is more than doubled. It is assured. This, after all, becomes the real reason for baking your own. It tastes better.

S.S.

BASIC RECIPES

Chicken Stock

Makes approximately 4 cups

1 lb. chicken legs
  (thigh plus leg)
5 C cold water
1 small carrot

1 small celery stalk
1 sprig parsley
salt to taste

1. Place chicken, water and vegetables in large soup kettle and bring to a boil.

2. Reduce heat. Boil slowly 45 minutes.

3. Salt to taste.

4. Strain off stock. Cool. Skim off all fat.

5. Strain again through a double layer of wet cheesecloth.

If a clearer stock is required, skim constantly while the stock is cooking.

Beef Stock

Makes approximately 3½ cups

1 lb. stewing beef
½ lb. beef marrow bones
5 C cold water
1 small carrot
1 small celery stalk

1 small onion, halved
1 bay leaf
2 sprigs parsley
3 black peppercorns
salt to taste

1. Brown half the meat in just enough oil to lightly coat the bottom of a heavy frying pan.

2. Remove browned meat and place it in a soup kettle with all other ingredients but salt and water.

3. Pour 5 C cold water into frying pan and scrape bottom with spoon to get off all the browned meat juices. Pour this into the soup kettle.

4. Bring to a boil. Reduce heat. Partially cover. Boil slowly 1½ hours or until meat is tender.

5. Salt to taste.

6. Strain. Cool stock. Skim off any fat and pour through a double layer of wet cheesecloth.

Searing the meat until it is dark brown will make the stock a darker color. However, browning meat seals in some of the juices. This is the reason why only half the meat is browned. Pour in ¼ cup of dry red wine at the beginning of cooking time if you have it on hand.

Fish Stock (Fumet)

Makes approximately 2 cups

1 lb. fish heads (gills removed),
 tails, bones, skin
1 small celery stalk
1 small onion, diced
 (or 3 shallots)

2½ C water
2 sprigs parsley
½ C dry vermouth
3 peppercorns
salt to taste

1. Combine all ingredients except salt in large sauce pan. Bring to a boil.

2. Reduce heat and boil slowly uncovered 15–20 minutes.

3. Salt to taste.

4. Strain through a double layer of wet cheesecloth.

Fish stock is strong and is used sparingly. Try a little in any seafood soup or casserole.

Pasta

Makes approximately 2 C cooked pasta

1 C unbleached all-purpose flour
1 egg (medium)
1 T olive oil

1 T cold water
dash of salt

1. Place flour on pastry board in a mound. Form a well.

2. Break egg into well and add oil and water. Add a dash or two of salt.

3. With floured fingers mix ingredients together. (Add extra flour if dough is too sticky to handle.)

4. Knead dough until it is elastic and smooth. Divide it into 3 parts.

5. Work each part through a pasta machine roller or roll out with a rolling pin until as thin as possible (less than $^1/_{16}$ inch).

6. Cut pasta into desired width and dry on baking sheets $^1/_2$–1 hour.

7. Drop into boiling water and boil until *al dente* (firm to the bite, not soft). This takes approximately 5–7 minutes.

The pasta may be either cooked in the soup broth or cooked separately and added to the soup last.

Basic White Bread

Makes 2 loaves

2 T yeast
¹/₂ C warm water
1¹/₂ C water
1 T salt (scant)

2 T corn oil
4¹/₂–5¹/₂ C unbleached
    all-purpose flour

1. Dissolve yeast in ¹/₂ C warm water.

2. Add water, salt, and oil.

3. Stir in 3 C flour. Beat 200 strokes.

4. Mix in 1¹/₂ C flour.

5. Knead 10 minutes, adding flour gradually to prevent sticking.

6. Brush with oil and cover. Let rise in oiled bowl until doubled in bulk (1¹/₂–2 hours).

7. Punch down. (Second rising is optional.) Cut in half. Round off and shape into loaves. Place in oiled bread pans. Cover. Let rise until doubled in bulk (45 minutes to 1 hour).

8. Bake at 400 degrees for 25–30 minutes. If tapping the bottom of the loaf produces a hollow sound, the bread is done. Remove from pans. Brush tops with butter. Cool on wire rack.

This water-based bread is failure proof. Its ingredients and method reflect the fundamentals of a wide range of yeasted loaves.

Glossary

Al Dente   An Italian term referring to pasta that is cooked firm to the bite.

Arrowroot   The powdered starchy root of a tropical plant. Used for thickening.

Bisque   A thick cream-based soup.

Blanch   To whiten food by pouring boiling water over it.

Blender   Kitchen machine composed of a glass or plastic container set over small electric-driven blades that liquefy food.

Bouillon   A strained, clear soup usually made from beef.

Bouquet garni   A bunch of fresh herbs tied together for easy removal before the dish is served.

Chowder   Thick fish or vegetable milk-based soup to which salt pork is usually added.

Consommé   A clarified brown stock made of beef or chicken.

Food mill   An implement on which a handle turns a blade that forces fruits and vegetables through perforations in a disc (the Foley Food Mills are well-known examples). Rices and purees.

Food processor   A multi-purpose electric kitchen machine that chops, mixes, blends, pulverizes when specifically designed blades are inserted.

Gumbo   A soup with a number of ingredients, but always thickened with okra.

Mezza luna   A half-moon shaped blade with handles on each end, good for chopping.

Purée   To blend or mash cooked food until it is of a smooth, thick consistency.

Roux   A mixture of equal amounts of melted butter and flour that is blended by cooking and then used to thicken sauces and soups.

Sauté   To fry lightly in oil or butter.

Scald   To heat a liquid to immediately below the boiling point.

Simmer   To cook in a liquid below the boiling point.

Stock   The liquid in which meat, poultry, fish, vegetables, or a combination of these has been cooked.

Soups & Breads

FOOD MILL

Artichoke Soup

Serves 5–7

2 T sweet butter
1/4 C flour
1 1/2 C milk
2 C artichoke hearts (4 large fresh,
  or two 9-oz. packages frozen)
1 T sweet butter
3 C chicken stock

1/4 t nutmeg
1/2 t lemon juice
salt and white pepper to taste

Garnish: generous amount of fresh minced
  parsley

1. Make a white sauce: melt 2 T butter, add flour. Stirring constantly with whisk, add milk, and cook over medium-low heat for 7–10 minutes until sauce is very thick.

2. At the same time sauté the artichoke hearts in 1 T butter. (Note: If hearts are frozen, cook according to directions first. If using fresh artichokes, boil them until they are easily punctured with a fork. Cut them into quarters and remove the hairy choke center. Remove thorny tips of leaves by cutting off the top. Leave the tender leaves on the hearts and slice.)

3. Work the artichoke hearts through the medium disc of a food mill.

4. Add the ground-up artichoke hearts and chicken broth to the white sauce and heat slowly.

5. Season soup with nutmeg, lemon juice, salt and pepper.

This soup has a delicate unusual flavor and makes an elegant appetizer for any roast. The frozen hearts are less trouble, but fresh artichokes produce a stronger flavor. Either way, this is a singular soup.

Young zinfandel

Sally Lunn

Makes 1 loaf

1 T yeast
1 C warm milk
³/₄ t salt
2 large eggs, beaten well

6 T melted sweet butter
2 T honey
3 C unbleached all-purpose flour

1. Dissolve yeast in warm milk. Add salt.

2. Beat eggs 1 minute.

3. To yeast add cooled melted butter, honey, and eggs.

4. Mix in 2 C flour. Beat 200 strokes. Add 1 C more flour and mix thoroughly. Dough will be very soft and sticky.

5. Cover and let rise in same bowl until doubled in bulk (1 hour or less).

6. Stir down. With oiled hands place or pour dough into buttered tube pan, large savarin mold, or large individual muffin tins. Let rise slightly (20–30 minutes).

7. Place in cold oven. Turn on heat to 350 degrees. Bake 30 minutes or until golden on top.

Served hot, Sally Lunn is unsurpassed as a delectable cake-like bread. This particular version is rich and buttery inside. It's best straight from the oven. Toasted for breakfast, it's manna.

Fruit salad

Asparagus–Cheese Soup

Serves 4 small portions

24 asparagus spears
1/2 C water
1/2 C dry white wine
2 T sweet butter
1 T flour
1 C milk

1 1/2 C grated mild Cheddar cheese
1 C light cream
salt and white pepper to taste

Garnish: *sprinkle of coriander*

1. To prepare fresh asparagus, cut off tough stalk base, leaving approximately 5 inches of the top of the spears. These may be pared of any tough outer fibers.

2. Bring the water and wine to a boil and drop in the spears at the same angle so that they cook evenly. Cover tightly and boil slowly for 7–10 minutes, until tender.

3. Melt butter and make a roux with the flour over medium-low heat. Add milk, stirring constantly. Do not boil.

4. Add the Cheddar cheese. Stir until the cheese is melted and remove the pan from the heat.

5. Drain the asparagus, reserving the liquid. On cutting board lay the spears all in the same direction in a row and cut off the tips (approximately 1 inch).

6. Using the finest disc work the rest of the stalks through a food mill, adding the asparagus liquid. (The food mill will strain out any particularly tough fibers, whereas the blender will merely chop them up finer.)

7. Add the asparagus purée to the cheese soup.

8. Cut the asparagus tips into 1/2-inch pieces and add to the soup. Add cream. Stir well and heat. Do not boil.

9. Salt and pepper to taste.

This soup is palatial. Asparagus has always been considered a delicacy and cheese is a natural companion. The problem with most asparagus soups is that they often are too strong. The wine and cheese refine this soup and adding only the tender asparagus tips avoids any stringiness. If it's the season, fresh is best, and wild even better. Use a good wine such as Fumé Blanc.

California Fumé Blanc

Anise Toast

1/2 C warm milk
4 T sweet butter
1 T yeast
1/4 C warm water
2 T honey
1/2 t salt

2 large eggs, slightly beaten
1 t fresh grated lemon rind
2 1/2 T anise seeds, crushed
1/2 t coriander
3 C unbleached all-purpose flour

1. Melt butter in heated milk. Cool.

2. Dissolve yeast in warm water. Add honey, salt, eggs, lemon rind, anise seeds, and coriander. Stir in buttermilk mixture.

3. Stir in 2 1/2 C flour. Beat well.

4. Knead dough for a few minutes. Dough will be soft. Add gradually 1/2 C more flour. If too sticky, add extra flour.

5. Place in oiled bowl and cover. Let rise until doubled in bulk (1 hour).

6. Punch down. Form into 1 long narrow French-like loaf. Place on lightly oiled baking sheet. Let rise until less than doubled.

7. Bake at 350 degrees for 25–30 minutes or until chestnut brown.

8. Cool. Slice and place on baking sheet. Toast in slow oven (200–250 degrees) for an hour or more, depending on thickness of slice. Toast both sides. Or toast lightly in toaster and let stand overnight on wire rack.

This bread may be eaten without toasting. It's rich, eggy, soft, and textured like a cake. Toasted and served warm with sweet butter melting all over, it's even better. Crush the anise seeds with a mortar and pestle or mash and cut them with a rolling pin and mezza luna. *Part of the pleasure of making this bread is the vibrant licorice aroma of anise lingering throughout the day.*

Fresh Boston lettuce salad with oil and basil vinegar dressing

Avgolemono Soup

Serves 4–6

6 C chicken stock
$^1/_3$ C white rice
2 eggs, beaten

$^1/_4$ C lemon juice
salt

Garnish: *thin lemon slices*

1. Bring the stock to a boil and pour in rice.

2. Cook covered at a slow boil for 15 minutes.

3. Beat eggs. (Another egg may be added if a thicker soup is preferred.) Whip lemon juice into eggs and, stirring constantly, very slowly add 2 C of hot broth to eggs.

4. Just before serving, add the egg mixture to the rice and chicken stock, stirring constantly over medium heat until hot but not boiling.

5. Salt to taste.

6. Let stand 5 minutes covered at side of stove.

Avgolemono is a favorite Greek soup. During her student days in service at a Greek-owned restaurant, this cook learned from George the Greek what a delicate and magnetic role a simple slice of lemon can play in a soup. Homemade bean, canned vegetable, it made no difference. The soup George served was always accompanied by a quarter of a fresh lemon.

Valpolicella

30

Poppy Seed Braid

1 T yeast
$^1/_4$ C warm water
2 t salt
$^1/_4$ C corn oil
2 T honey
$^3/_4$ C warm milk

2 eggs, slightly beaten
4-plus C unbleached all-purpose flour
5 t poppy seeds
1 egg yolk
1 T water

1. Dissolve yeast in warm water in separate small bowl.

2. Place salt, oil, honey, milk in large bowl. Stir to dissolve.

3. Add beaten eggs. Add yeast.

4. Stir in 3 C flour and beat 200 strokes. Add 1 more C flour.

5. Knead. Add extra flour to keep from sticking. (Possibly $^1/_4$–$^1/_2$ C may be needed.)

6. In oiled bowl cover and let rise for 2 hours.

7. Punch down. Divide into 3 equal parts.

8. Roll each part out into long narrow strip 4 inches wide. Sprinkle $1^1/_2$ t poppy seeds evenly on each strip. Roll up lengthwise and pinch edges. (The poppy seeds are on the inside.)

9. Lay 3 long ropes of dough side by side and braid them loosely. Pinch and tuck ends underneath. Place on large oiled baking sheet.

10. Cover and let rise 1 hour. With fingers apply French wash of egg yolk mixed with water. Sprinkle liberally with poppy seeds.

11. Bake 25–30 minutes at 375.

The overdose of oil in this bread results in a satiny texture. The buried swirls of poppy seeds add another surprise. The crust will be a rich deep shiny brown with lighter shades in the crevices of the braid. A yellower interior may be produced by adding another egg–with slightly more flour to compensate for the extra moisture. A pinch of saffron will also deepen the color.

Tossed salad with Feta cheese

Avocado Soup (Cold)

Serves 4

1 1/2 C avocado
2 1/2 C chicken stock (more for a
  thinner consistency)
2 t lemon juice
1/8 t Tabasco sauce

1 t grated onion
salt

Garnish: yellow-orange nasturtium
  (or squash) blossoms

1. Halve avocado(s) and scoop out pulp.
2. Place all ingredients with avocado in blender. Purée well.
3. Chill soup thoroughly in blender container.
4. Serve in chilled white or clear glass bowls.

At most, cold avocado soup takes 3 minutes to prepare, and its original flavor is sure to spark favorable comment. Beatrice Trum Hunter, author of Food Additives and Your Health, *informed us that California avocado crops have been cultivated for years using very few pesticides. From the start, growers introduced biological pest control in the groves, making this a safe fruit to eat without worrying about toxins.*

Mexican beer

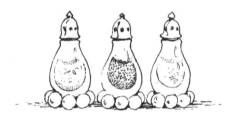

Wheat Flat Bread

1 T toasted sesame seeds
1/2 C whole wheat flour
1/2 C unbleached all-purpose flour

1/2 t salt
1/2 C water (scant)

1. Toast sesame seeds in skillet until dark tan. Some will pop and jump.

2. Mix whole wheat and white flours, salt, and toasted sesame seeds.

3. Stir in water. Knead a few minutes until smooth in texture.

4. Divide with knife into 6 equal pieces.

5. Roll each piece into as thin a circle possible on floured board.

6. Cook each on both sides in ungreased iron skillet over medium heat until light brown spots appear (approximately 1/2–1 1/2 minutes).

Serve warm. While the rest are being cooked, the first may be kept warm in the oven and then wrapped all together in a cloth napkin in a bread basket.

Flat bread is good with butter and eaten folded. Or, for a more elaborate meal, a favorite of ours is chamoles, *a term we coined from* chapattis *(a lighter flat bread) and* guacamole *(an avocado-based spread). Serve* chamoles *rolled up with grated mild cheese, pieces of broiled bacon, and spicy* guacamole.

Monterey Jack cheese

Beef–Espresso Consommé

Serves 8–12

2 T corn oil
1 lb. stewing beef
1 small onion, quartered
1/2 lb. beef marrow bones
3/4 lb. shank veal cutlets
   (with bone in)
3 peppercorns
1 clove
12 C water

1 end celery stalk with leaves
1 sprig parsley
1 small carrot
2/3 C espresso coffee, freshly brewed
salt to taste
1 egg white and shell

Garnish: *thin lemon slices*

1. Place large heavy frying pan coated with oil over medium heat.

2. Brown the stewing beef and onion until both are very dark (on the verge of burnt).

3. Place marrow bones, veal, peppercorns, clove, browned beef and onion in a large heavy soup pot and cover with cold water. Slowly bring to a boil. (The slower this process the more juices are drawn from the meats.)

4. Add celery, parsley, and carrot.

5. During the first 1/2 hour skim the fat and scum off the top. Usually for nutritive value this is not done, but for a clear consommé it is advisable.

6. Cover the broth and cook at an excruciatingly slow boil for not less than 3 hours.

7. Strain off the broth and retain the meats for a delicious stew or main course. Place a double thick layer of wet cheesecloth in a large strainer and pour the broth through.

8. Add coffee. Salt to taste.

9. Refrigerate so that the fat congeals and may be removed.

10. To clarify 4 C consommé, place 1 egg white and crushed egg shell in 1 quart of cold consommé.

11. Bring the consommé to a boil, beating constantly with a whisk. Simmer covered 1/2 hour. Skim.

12. Strain the consommé through a strainer lined with wet double cheesecloth.

This clear dark consommé with a distinctive flavor is an elegant appetizer or light refreshment. The browning of the meat and the coffee enhance the dark rich brown color and taste. Clarifying consommé is a magical process as surprising and gratifying as developing pictures. If you haven't done it, try it and witness the miracle firsthand.

Pinot noir

Croissants

¹/₄ lb. slightly softened sweet butter
2 T flour
³/₄ C warm milk
1 T yeast
¹/₂ t salt

2 C unbleached all-purpose flour
egg yolk wash (1 yolk mixed
with 1 T water)

1. Cream butter and 2 T flour. Refrigerate 10 minutes.

2. Dissolve yeast in milk in large bowl. Add salt.

3. Stir in 1 C flour and beat 200 strokes. Add rest of flour.

4. Knead until elastic and smooth (approximately 10 minutes).

5. Roll dough to 10 × 7-inch rectangle.

6. Flatten butter to slightly less than ¹/₃ the size of the dough rectangle. Place butter over center third of dough. Fold long sides of dough inward ¹/₂ inch. Then fold each end third over center third. Cover dough and refrigerate for 20 minutes.

7. Roll dough into ¹/₄-inch thick rectangle. Fold ends over center third again. Refrigerate if butter oozes out when rolling. Repeat this step 3 times in succession. Work fast.

8. Finally, roll out to an exact 6 × 18-inch rectangle. Cut into three 6-inch squares. Cut each square into 2 triangles.

9. By hand roll very loosely from long side of triangle. Place end point on bottom. Stretch lengthwise slightly and curve ends inward, almost touching, to form crescent.

10. Place well apart on lightly oiled baking surface, preferably glass. Chill 10–15 minutes.

11. Brush with egg yolk wash. Bake for approximately 15 minutes at 375 degrees or until golden. Serve warm.

Croissants are such extraordinary butter-rich, flaky rolls that they should be made frequently. Unfortunately, most recipes take 6 or more hours. We've relied on good high-gluten flour, beating to stretch it, kneading, and especially the butter–air separation of the layers of dough to offset the two risings often called for. We encourage everyone to try these and not be put off by the tradition of their difficulty. You do need to get the feel of working with croissants, but keep at it. This recipe is as simple as we can get it, and should take under 3 hours from yeast to yummy.

Gervais cheese

Black Bean Soup

1 C black beans
¹/₈ lb. salt pork, blanched
2 C chicken stock
1 ripe medium-size tomato, diced
4 C cold water
2 cloves garlic, crushed and minced
¹/₂ C diced onion

¹/₄ t hot pepper (dried, jalapeña sauce,
*   or preserved whole chilis)*
¹/₂ t oregano
1 ¹/₂ T olive oil
salt and pepper
2 T dry sherry

Garnish: *sour cream*

1. Wash and presoak beans 2–3 hours.

2. To blanch salt pork, cover it with boiling water and let stand a few minutes.

3. Place beans, salt pork, chicken stock, tomato, and cold water in large soup pot. Bring to boil. Reduce heat and cover. Cook at slow boil for 1¹/₂–2 hours.

4. Sauté garlic, onion, red pepper or chili, and oregano in olive oil until onion is golden. Add mixture to beans. Salt and pepper soup to taste.

5. Reserve 1 C whole cooked beans. Purée remaining soup in a blender.

6. Reheat *all* ingredients together 5 minutes. Stir in sherry.

7. Ladle into bowls and float a dollop of sour cream in each.

Black bean soup is striking served in everyday white bowls. Mexican pottery and bright napkins also offset the black bean, a color which rarely appears in nature. The chili content is at the cook's discretion. As they say of Mexican food, you eat with your right hand and wipe your nose with your left.

Mexican beer

Sopapillas

1 C unbleached all-purpose flour
1 t baking powder
1/4 t salt

1 T sweet butter
1/3 C water
corn oil for deep frying

1. Mix flour, baking powder, and salt.

2. Cut in butter. Stir in water.

3. Knead 5 minutes. Cover and let rest 15–20 minutes.

4. Roll into a rectangle that measures 6 × 12 inches and less than 1/8 inch thick. Cut away excess dough to make straight edges.

5. With ruler measure 3-inch squares and cut.

6. Deep fry squares very briefly in hot oil (375 degrees) until they puff and are light golden on both sides. Place on absorbent paper. Serve warm.

Santa Fe is the home of these golden fried puff breads and at La Tertulia *restaurant we saw what tantalizing works of art they can be. If you cut* sopapillas *all in the same size and shape and fry them to the same color, they'll come out an attractive basketful of tiny pillows.* Sopapillas *must be made immediately before serving; they don't keep well. For a yellowish interior and more bread-like texture, add an egg to the above recipe and cut the water approximately in half. Without the egg, this recipe produces a cloud-light golden pouch of steam. Break off a corner and slip some honeybutter inside, the traditional—and practical—way of eating them.*

Honeybutter

Blue Cheese Soup

Serves 8

1 lb. stewing beef
8 C water
1 T basil
1 T minced parsley
1 ½ C cooked homemade or commercial
  German-type egg noodles

2 oz. blue or Roquefort cheese
salt to taste
½ t freshly ground black pepper

Garnish: *extra blue cheese*

1. Place stew meat in a large pot, cover with water, and bring to a boil.

2. Add basil and parsley.

3. Lower the heat and cook covered at a slow boil for 3 hours.

4. Cook the noodles separately. Drain and add them to the beef broth.

5. Salt and add ½ t pepper.

6. The blue cheese goes in last, and cooks just long enough to melt completely. Do not boil.

Blue cheese lovers may crumble more into their soup at the table. And those who think blue cheese tastes like soap will find the flavor of this soup mild, creamy, and appetizing.

Petite Sirah red wine

Pumpernickel

1 C espresso coffee, freshly brewed
2 T yeast
3 T blackstrap molasses
1¹/₂ t salt
1 T corn oil
1 large egg, slightly beaten

³/₄ T caraway seeds
¹/₂ C buckwheat flour
1 C rye flour
2¹/₄ C graham flour
yellow cornmeal

1. In warm (not hot) coffee, dissolve yeast.

2. Add molasses, salt, oil, egg, caraway seeds.

3. Stir in buckwheat, rye, 1 C graham flours. Beat 200 strokes.

4. Add rest of graham flour. Knead 15 minutes, adding extra graham flour as needed to prevent sticking. Dough will be stiff and sticky. Cover and let rise until doubled in bulk (2 hours).

5. Punch down and knead a few minutes. Round into a mounded oval loaf and place on an oiled baking sheet lightly sprinkled with yellow cornmeal. Cover and let rise until nearly doubled in bulk (1 hour).

6. With razor blade, cut a checker pattern of 3 lines crossing 3 others 1 inch deep. If you have extra coffee, brush top with it.

7. Bake at 375 degrees for 45 minutes or until tapping the bottom of the loaf produces a hollow sound. Brush with butter and cool on wire rack.

This version produces a hardy, crunchy crust with a softish center. Dark and heavy, this bread has the taste of outdoors, a sturdy stick-to-the-ribs bread. A lot of kneading is necessary for this one because of the low gluten content in the buckwheat and rye flours.

Blue cheese

Borscht (Cold)

2 C diced beets
  (7–8 medium-size beets)
2 1/2 C beet liquid
1 C beef stock or bouillon
1 T grated onion
1 T lemon juice

1/2 t salt

Garnish: sliced hard-boiled eggs
  (1/2 egg per person); peeled,
  sliced cucumber; sour cream

1. Scrub beets and cut stems no shorter than 1 inch from the top so that the beets won't bleed.

2. In water to cover boil beets until tender (approximately 45 minutes). Eggs may be boiled in same pan and removed after 20 minutes.

3. Save beet water. Drain beets and place them in cold water. Slip off skins.

4. Add 2 1/2 C beet water to 1 C beef stock or bouillon.

5. Blend 1 C beets with 1 C beef–beet liquid. Repeat with other cup of beets.

6. Stir blended beets and remaining liquid together. Add onion, lemon juice, and salt.

7. Chill at least 2 hours in pitcher in refrigerator.

8. Stir borscht well before pouring into bowls.

9. Float cucumber and egg slices on top of each serving and crown with a dollop of sour cream.

One hot day a sophisticated New York poet invited this Midwesterner, then a naive student, to lunch. "Do you like borscht?" she asked. "Oh, sure!" She combined the above ingredients, and borscht has impressed ever since. The magenta of garden-fresh beets, the yellow eyes of the eggs, and the crisp green tinge of cucumber are psychedelic colors and tastes. The beet greens may be saved, washed, and cooked down with diced bacon and a little vinegar.

Stout

Rye Bread

2 T yeast
¹/₂ C warm water
1 C water
1 T blackstrap molasses
¹/₂ T salt
2 T corn oil
1 T malt

2 t caraway seeds
2¹/₂ C rye flour
2 C unbleached all-purpose flour
yellow cornmeal
sesame seeds

1. In a large bowl dissolve yeast in ½ C warm water.

2. Mix in 1 C water, molasses, salt, oil, malt, caraway seeds.

3. Stir in rye flour. Beat 3–4 minutes.

4. Add 1³/₄ C all-purpose flour. Mix well.

5. Knead dough at least 15 minutes, preferably 20, on a bread board. Add approximately ¹/₄ C all-purpose flour gradually as needed to eliminate sticky dough.

6. Place in oiled bowl, cover, and let rise until doubled in bulk (2–3 hours).

7. Punch down and shape into loaf. Oil bread pan and sprinkle bottom with cornmeal.

8. Place dough in pan to rise until doubled in bulk (approximately 1–2 hours).

9. With razor blade slice down center of loaf approximately 1 inch deep. Brush top with water and sprinkle a pinch of sesame seeds on top.

10. Place in cold oven. Turn heat to 400 degrees and bake for 30–35 minutes. Remove from pan and brush top with butter. Cool on wire rack.

Rye takes more kneading to stretch its low content of gluten, so be sure to work the dough at least 15 minutes. This recipe produces an amber-colored loaf with a characteristic hardy rye flavor.

São Jorge cheese

Broccoli–Tahini Soup

2 heaping C broccoli flowers
water to cover and 2 T lemon juice
3 C chicken stock
1 C water

3 T sesame tahini
1 t lemon juice
salt to taste

Garnish: *toasted sesame seeds*

1. Cut broccoli flowers from stems. Cover flowers with cold water and 2 T lemon juice. Weight down with plate. Soak.

2. Drain broccoli and place in soup pot with chicken stock and 1 C water.

3. Bring broccoli to a boil. Lower heat and boil slowly, covered, until flowers are bright green but tender.

4. Pour off 2 C of the liquid. Cool and place in blender with tahini. (Or beat a little liquid at a time into the tahini with a whisk.) Blend.

5. Return tahini mixture to pot.

6. Add 1 t lemon juice and salt to taste.

7. Reheat and serve at once.

Sesame tahini is made of ground hulled sesame seeds and may usually be found in health food stores. The sesame oil tends to separate from the paste, so stir the tahini well before using. If tahini is added to the hot stock without blending or beating in slowly, it will curdle. Soaking the broccoli will bring out any little creatures hiding in the spears. By cooking the broccoli in the stock you retain its vitamins. And since tahini is extra rich in protein and calcium, this is one soup that is both exotic and healthy.

Orange Pekoe tea

Toasted Wheat Berry Muffins

1/4 C toasted and ground wheat berries
1 T yeast
1/4 C warm water
2 T corn oil
2 T honey
1/2 t salt

2 eggs, slightly beaten
3/4 C warm milk
1 1/2 C unbleached all-purpose flour
1/4 C yellow cornmeal

1. Toast wheat berries. Grind them finely in a blender.

2. Dissolve yeast in water.

3. Stir oil, honey, salt, and eggs into milk.

4. Add flour, cornmeal, wheat berries. Mix thoroughly but briefly.

5. Fill oiled muffin cups 2/3 full.

6. Place in cold oven. Turn heat to 400 degrees. Bake about 20 minutes or until lightly browned.

If you like a bold brown nutty taste to your breads, you'll like these. Whole wheat berries are found at most natural food stores. Toast them by spreading them in an iron frying pan over medium heat. In a couple of minutes a few will pop. Stir them with a wooden spoon and spread them out by shaking the pan as you would a popcorn popper. Toast them to your taste—the darker the nuttier. Not only do the berries add a robust taste but they're also highly nutritious because they are the whole unprocessed wheat kernels.

Cottage cheese

Chick Pea Soup

6 C water
2 C chicken stock
3¹/₂ C cooked chick peas
¹/₂ C diced onion
1 large whole ripe tomato,
    peeled and cored
1 bay leaf
1 t minced parsley
6 cloves garlic, crushed

¹/₈ t hot red pepper sauce
1 T olive oil
1 lb. fresh spinach, washed, drained,
    de-stemmed, chopped finely
2 t wine vinegar
salt to taste

Garnish: *grated Parmesan cheese*

1. Cooking dried chick peas takes a great deal of time. They must be soaked overnight and then cooked at a slow boil in water to cover (adding water as they cook) until they are tender (usually 2–3 hours). Precooked chick peas are available and easier. Wash and drain them.

2. Mix the water and chicken stock in a large soup pot and bring it to a boil.

3. Add 1¹/₂ C chick peas, onion, tomato, bay leaf, parsley, 4 garlic cloves, and hot pepper.

4. Lower heat so soup cooks at a gentle boil and cook covered 45 minutes.

5. Strain out the vegetables. Discard the bay leaf. Purée the vegetables with olive oil and 2 uncooked cloves of garlic through the fine disc of a food mill or in a blender.

6. Return the chick pea mixture to the broth and stir it in.

7. Add the spinach and cook another 15 minutes.

8. Add the remaining 2 C of whole chick peas and vinegar last. Salt to taste.

This soup is simple but has a healthy peasant taste. Chick peas or garbanzos *may usually be found in the Italian section of your supermarket.*

Cold milk

Soy Bread

Makes 1 large loaf

1 T yeast
¹/₄ C warm water
1 T corn oil
1 T blackstrap molasses
1 t salt
1 egg, slightly beaten

¹/₃ C dry milk
1 C water
¹/₄ C soy flour
¹/₄ C wheat germ
1 C whole wheat flour
2¹/₄ C unbleached all-purpose flour

1. In bread bowl dissolve yeast in warm water.

2. Add oil, molasses, salt, egg, dry milk, water. Stir.

3. Mix in soy, wheat germ, whole wheat and 1 C all-purpose flour. Beat 200 strokes.

4. Add 1 C all-purpose flour. Knead 10 minutes, adding ¹/₄–¹/₃ C more all-purpose flour as needed to prevent sticking.

5. Cover and let rise in oiled bowl (1–1¹/₂ hours).

6. Punch down. Shape into loaf and place in oiled bread pan. Cover and let rise until slightly less than doubled in bulk (1 hour).

7. Bake at 375 degrees for 25–30 minutes or until done. Remove from pan, brush with butter, and cool on wire rack.

You can live by bread alone, provided it's soy bread. Cornell University developed the basic soybean flour loaf (hence the alternative name "Cornell Bread") as a total nourishing food. The triple-rich ingredients, as they're called, are soy flour, dry milk, and wheat germ, all of which together provide the necessary nutrients to sustain life. Soy flour is made from grinding cooked, dried soybeans (which are legumes, not grass as wheat is) and contains up to 40% protein and all the essential amino acids. This bread is ideal for people who don't have access to meat. This recipe bakes into a high, light, nut-brown loaf.

Leicester cheese

Chicken Gumbo

Serves 6–8

3 rashers bacon, diced
2 chicken breasts, split
4 C water
4 C 1-inch pieces okra
   (or two 10-oz. boxes frozen)
1/2 C diced green pepper
1/3 C diced onion
1 T minced parsley

2 C whole peeled tomatoes and juice
1/3 C tomato paste
1/2 lb. ham steak, diced
1/4 lb. deveined shrimp
salt to taste
1/2 t Louisiana hot sauce (Tabasco)

Garnish: fluffy steamed white rice

1. Fry bacon in large iron frying pan. Pour off half the fat along with the bacon pieces and retain half the fat in the pan.

2. Dredge the chicken in flour and fry in the bacon fat until brown.

3. Cover the chicken with 4 C water and cook at slow boil for 20 minutes.

4. Dice the vegetables. (Frozen okra need not be cooked before it is cut.) In large heavy soup pot sauté all the vegetables except the tomatoes in the remaining bacon fat with bacon pieces for 10 minutes.

5. Add tomatoes and tomato paste.

6. Drain the chicken and pour the broth into the soup pot with the vegetables.

7. Remove chicken from the bones and tear it into bite-size shreds.

8. Dice the ham and cut the shrimp into bite-size pieces.

9. Add the ham, shrimp, and chicken to soup pot.

10. Bring the gumbo to a boil and boil slowly, covered, for 1 hour.

11. Salt to taste and add the hot sauce last.

12. Pass around a bowl of rice or place a scoop of rice in the center of each bowl.

Gumbo is a Southern Creole dish. Many recipes call for filé *powder, which is a thickening agent made from sassafras. The powder is now banned as a carcinogen. If you like extra thick soup, a tablespoon of arrowroot or two tablespoons corn starch may be mixed with a little water and stirred into the soup. However, we've found that the okra itself thickens the soup without the addition of starches.*

Lime cooler

Buttermilk–Bacon Spoon Bread

Makes 6 servings

3 thick slices lean bacon
1 large egg, separated
2 C buttermilk
1 T honey

1 C yellow cornmeal
1 1/2 t baking soda
1/2 t salt (scant)

1. Broil bacon until crisp and reserve fat.

2. Beat egg white into stiff peaks.

3. Heat to lukewarm: buttermilk, slightly beaten egg yolk, honey, 1 T reserved bacon fat.

4. In large bowl combine cornmeal, baking soda, salt, crisp bacon crushed into bits.

5. Add buttermilk mixture. Fold in egg whites.

6. Heat 1 1/2-quart casserole dish greased with bacon fat. Pour in the ingredients.

7. Bake at 350 degrees for 15–20 minutes. Do not overbake.

Spoon bread is pudding-like, scooped out and eaten with a spoon. This version is smooth and lip-smacking good. It's quick to make but must be served straight from the oven. Overcooking will make it sliceable, just as tasty but not spoon bread Southern style.

Homemade pimento cheese (cream cheese and chopped pimentos) on top of hot spoon bread

47

Chicken Leg Noodle Soup

Serves 4

4 chicken legs (with thighs)
10 C water
1 large celery stalk with leaves

2 C thin egg noodles
salt to taste

Garnish: minced fresh scallions

1. In a large soup pot cover the legs with water (allow $2^1/_2$ C water for each chicken leg and 1 leg per person). Add celery.

2. Bring to a fast boil. Reduce heat to a slow boil. Cover and cook 1 hour.

3. Salt broth to taste. (Chicken soup takes a lot of salt.)

4. Remove legs and celery stalk. Take the meat off the legs, discarding skin and bones.

5. Put the chicken meat back in broth. Bring to a boil and add the noodles.

6. Reduce heat to medium and boil the soup uncovered 7–10 minutes or until the noodles are al dente.

Chicken soup is proverbial. If it did everything it was supposed to, it would replace the medical profession. If you're poor, eat the soup minus the meat one meal and the legs the next meal. If you're rich, go "whole chicken."

Cold milk

Sage Biscuits

1 C unbleached all-purpose flour
1/4 t salt
1 1/2 t baking powder
1 T minced sage leaves

2 t chopped parsley
2 T sweet butter
6 T milk

1. Mix flour, salt, baking powder, sage, and parsley.

2. Cut in butter until mealy.

3. Add milk 1 T at a time, gently stirring it in each time with a fork.

4. Pat dough together carefully. Then pat gently onto board to 1/2 inch thickness. Shape into biscuits with 2-inch cutter.

5. Place on ungreased sheet or pie plate. Bake at 450 degrees for 12 minutes or until golden.

Be sure to use sage leaves. Using ground sage misses the point of this recipe and will produce gray biscuits. One tablespoon of leaves gives a distinct sage taste. Reduce to two teaspoons if you prefer a milder aroma and taste. Also, don't use a rolling pin, only your hands—and with as little pressure as possible. The outcome will be light, earthy-smelling biscuits.

Sweet butter and honey

Cock-a-Leekie Soup

Serves 4–6

4–5 veal bones
10 C water
1 lb. chicken pieces (leg plus
  thigh is tastier than breasts)
1 small carrot
1 small celery stalk
1 small onion

salt and white pepper to taste
3 leeks (white part only)
  (approximately 2 C thinly sliced)
8 dried apricots, cooked
8 prunes, cooked, pitted, halved

Garnish: orange twists

1. Place veal bones in soup pot and cover with cold water.

2. Bring to a boil, reduce heat, and cook at slow boil for 1 hour.

3. Strain veal stock through a double layer of wet cheesecloth.

4. Wash the pot of any scum and add veal stock, chicken, carrot, celery, onion.

5. Cook covered at a slow boil for 1 hour.

6. Strain out the vegetables and chicken, reserving the stock.

7. Let chicken cool. Discard skin and bones and cut chicken meat into bite-size pieces.

8. Skim fat off the stock.

9. Return the chicken meat and stock to the pot. Salt and pepper to taste.

10. Cut white part of leeks into 1/4-inch slices. Add the leeks to soup and boil for 7–10 minutes or until they are soft.

11. The prunes and apricots may be added to the soup in the kitchen or passed around the table. (To prepare them, soak overnight, cover with water, and boil covered for approximately 10 minutes.)

Since Medieval cookbooks often combine fruits and broths, this Scotch recipe must be an old castle favorite. The addition of the leek was introduced to Scotland by the French. Cock-a-leekie has a delightful taste, the tart apricot–prune flavors against the smooth salty chicken–veal stock.

Apricot juice

Raisin Bread

Makes 1 loaf

BREAD:
1 T yeast
1 C warm milk
1 t salt
1 T corn oil
2 C unbleached all-purpose flour

FILLING:
2 T melted sweet butter
1/4 C dark brown sugar
2 t cinnamon
1 t coriander
1/2 C raisins

ICING:
1/3 C confectioners' sugar
2–3 t water
1/4 t almond extract

1. Dissolve yeast in warm milk. Add salt and oil.

2. Stir in flour 1 C at a time. Knead for 10 minutes.

3. Cover and let rise until doubled in bulk (1 1/2 hours).

4. Punch down. Knead a minute or two.

5. Roll out to thin rectangle 10 inches wide. Brush with melted butter.

6. Mix sugar, cinnamon, and coriander, and sprinkle on dough. Sprinkle on raisins.

7. From narrow side, roll dough tightly. Tuck ends underneath. Pinch the long edge closed. Place seam down on lightly oiled baking sheet.

8. Cover. Let rise until nearly doubled in bulk (1 hour).

9. Bake at 350 degrees for 25–30 minutes or until golden brown. Cool on wire rack.

10. Mix confectioners' sugar, water, and almond extract so that it's relatively thin. Brush on slightly cooled loaf.

By rolling the dough thin, you end up with more of what this basic loaf is designed to have —raisins coated with butter, spices, and sugar. Sometimes we add a layer of sliced peeled Northern Spy apples for a different taste. (If you do this, increase the baking time to compensate for the moisture in the apples or the inside dough won't cook thoroughly.)

Chilled sliced pears

Corn–Scallop Chowder

Serves 4

4 C water
1 lb. scallops
2 T sweet butter
1 C diced onions
1/2 C diced celery
1 T flour
1 C diced potatoes

1 bay leaf
salt and white pepper to taste
2 C milk
1/2 C sour cream
1 C kernel corn, drained

Garnish: minced sweet red pepper

1. Bring water to boil. If using large sea scallops, cut into bite-size pieces. Add scallops to water and simmer for 5 minutes.

2. Strain the liquid (reserve) and retain scallops in a bowl.

3. Return scallop liquid to the heat and reduce by boiling to 2 C.

4. Melt butter in a large heavy pot or frying pan. Sauté onions and celery in butter. Stir in flour.

5. Add scallop liquid, 1/2 C cooked scallops, potatoes, bay leaf, salt and white pepper.

6. Simmer, covered, until potatoes are tender. Remove bay leaf.

7. Heat milk separately until tepid and whisk in sour cream. (Note: If milk gets too hot, sour cream will curdle.)

8. Add this milk mixture to the soup pot along with remaining scallops and corn.

9. Taste chowder again for salt and pepper.

This chowder is filling and notable for the textures of crisp corn kernels which offset the chewy bite-size pieces of scallops. If you're lucky enough to get them, the smaller, flavorful New England bay scallops may be left uncut.

Ale

Hush Puppies

Makes 12–16

1 C coarse yellow cornmeal
1/3 C unbleached all-purpose flour
3/4 t salt
1 t baking powder

1/4 C loosely packed minced onion
3/4 C milk
corn oil, at least 1 C

1. Mix cornmeal, flour, salt, baking powder.

2. Add onions to milk.

3. Combine dry and wet mixtures and stir.

4. Heat corn oil to 365 degrees or to smoking point.

5. Flatten heaping tablespoonful of dough by hand into ovals 1/4 to 1/2 inch thick.

6. Deep fry until brown (less than a minute). Dab with paper towels and place in aluminum foil-lined bread basket. Serve warm.

The oft-told tale is that these fried cornmeal tidbits came from Southern fishermen quieting their hounds by throwing them some and shouting, "Hush, puppies!" True or not, hush puppies are quick to make and savory besides. Fine yellow cornmeal works, but rough-cut stone-ground meal makes them a little more back-country. You don't need a deep fryer for these; an ordinary deep saucepan will do. We use a wok for small supplies of fried breads.

Cooper cheese

53

Cucumber Soup (Cold)

Serves 4–6

½ C diced shallots or onions
3 T sweet butter
3½ C cucumber, peeled, seeded and
   cut into ½-inch pieces
6 C chicken broth
2 t wine vinegar

1 t dried dill
salt and white pepper to taste
½ C sour cream

Garnish: *fresh mint sprigs*

1. Sauté shallots (or onions) in butter until golden and soft.

2. Add cucumber, broth, vinegar, and dill.

3. Boil slowly covered ½ hour until cucumber is soft.

4. Purée the soup in a blender.

5. Add salt and white pepper to taste.

6. Whisk sour cream into warm soup.

7. Chill in a pitcher in refrigerator for at least 3 hours.

8. Pour into chilled bowls and serve with a sprig of mint floating in center of each.

Cold cucumber soup served in chilled glass bowls is easy to prepare and effortless to eat on hot do-nothing days as a brunch, a light elegant lunch, or high tea. A simple garden salad of Romaine lettuce and tomatoes would add a nuance of color and crispness to the meal.

Vin Mousseux (sparkling dry white wine)

Popovers

1 C milk, heated to lukewarm
1 1/2 T melted sweet butter
1 large egg at room temperature and
    slightly beaten
7/8 C unbleached all-purpose flour
1/4 t salt

1. Heat milk and melt butter. Cool.

2. Add egg to cooled butter and milk.

3. Mix flour and salt.

4. Combine flour and liquid.

5. Heat large oiled muffin tins.

6. Fill hot tins half full.

7. Bake 20 minutes at 450 degrees. Reduce oven to 350 degrees and bake 15–20 minutes more.

After many experiments, we've found that one large egg and the proportions above are all you need for an elegant set of high-rise, thin-wall, crusty and custardy, nut-brown popovers. These American creations require immediate heat, so warm the milk slightly if it has been in the refrigerator, and have the egg at room temperature. The melted butter must be cooled or the egg will curdle. When you pour the batter into the hot, not merely warm, tins, it should sizzle. After the popovers are baked, wrap them in a cloth napkin and serve steaming hot. Popovers have a temperamental reputation which this recipe should cure. They make a widely adaptable addition to any breakfast, lunch, or dinner.

Sweet butter and wild grape jelly

Dry Soup

¹/₄ C corn oil
6 oz. very thin egg noodles or vermicelli
    broken into 2-inch pieces
¹/₄ C diced onion
2 cloves garlic, minced
2 C whole peeled tomatoes and juice

1 t jalapeña pepper sauce or
   ¹/₂ t hot crushed red pepper
1 C chicken stock
¹/₄ t oregano
salt and pepper to taste

Garnish: *grated Romano or Parmesan cheese*

1. Place oil in wok or large heavy frying pan over medium heat.

2. Sauté noodles until golden brown.

3. Remove noodles with a slotted spoon, leaving as much oil in the pan as possible.

4. Sauté onion and garlic in remaining oil 5 minutes.

5. Add tomatoes, pepper sauce, noodles, and chicken stock. Cover. Finish cooking soup in the heavy frying pan with tight lid.

6. Cook soup until it is nearly dry (30 minutes) over low heat.

7. Serve dry soup with grated cheese.

Sopa seca *or dry soup is an amusing contradiction in terms.* Mexicans *prepare* sopa seca *out of anything: noodles, tortillas, bread. South of the border, stale tortillas are the handiest common denominator.*

Mexican beer

56

Pan Dulce

1 T yeast
$^1/_2$ C warm water
$^1/_2$ C honey
3 C unbleached all-purpose flour
$^1/_2$ t salt
2 t anise seed
3 T melted sweet butter
2 eggs, slightly beaten

TOPPING:
$^3/_4$ C sugar
5 T melted sweet butter
1 egg, slightly beaten
$^3/_4$ C flour
$^1/_2$ t coriander
$^1/_2$ t cinnamon

1. Dissolve yeast in water. Add honey. Stir.

2. Add salt and anise seed to flour. Then add butter, 2 eggs, yeast. Mix thoroughly. Dough will be stiff.

3. Place in oiled bowl, cover, and let rise until doubled in bulk (approximately $1^1/_2$–2 hours).

4. Punch down. Knead until smooth on lightly floured board (5–10 minutes).

5. Pinch off pieces 2 inches in diameter. Round off and place on lightly oiled baking sheet. Leave room for expansion of buns.

6. Make topping by combining and mixing all ingredients in one step.

7. Press rolls flat with heel of your hand. Spread 1–$1^1/_2$ T topping on center of each bun. Let rise approximately $^1/_2$ hour.

8. Bake at 350 degrees for 10–12 minutes or until sides are slightly browned.

The topping stays on the dome of the rolls as they rise and bake. These are deceptively plain looking buns but they're delicious and rich. Mexicans serve them hot for breakfast. North of the border these buns are equally devourable for lunch or tea. The anise seed in the dough adds a subtle pungent flavor against the faint sweetish coriander in the topping.

Monterey Jack hot pepper cheese

Duck Soup

1 4–5 lb. duck cut into pieces
   trimmed of excess fat
1/2 C wild rice
bouquet garni (3 shallots,
   3 sprigs parsley, 1 bay leaf,
   1/2 t marjoram, 1/2 t sage leaves,
   3 peppercorns all tied in piece
   of cheesecloth)
2 C apple cider
4 C good Burgundy wine

4 C water
1 T arrowroot dissolved in 1/2 C cold water
1/8 t mace
salt and pepper
1 jigger hard cider (if not
   available, a jigger of brandy,
   jigger of beer, or both mixed)

Garnish: orange twists

1. In a large pot place the duck on top of the rice. Put in the bouquet garni and cover with cider and Burgundy.

2. Bring to a boil. Reduce heat to a slow boil, cover, and cook 2 hours.

3. With a slotted spoon transfer the pieces of duck to a bowl. Cool.

4. Strain out the rice, removing the bouquet garni. Run water through rice to rinse off any fat.

5. The broth will have a layer of fat. To make skimming easier, place broth in the freezer compartment. It will set in approximately 1/2 hour. Skim solidified fat off top of the broth and return broth to soup pot.

6. After duck has cooled, pick all meat off the bones and cut or shred it into small bite-size pieces.

7. Add rice and duck meat to soup along with 4 C water. Cook another 15 minutes to blend taste.

8. Dissolve arrowroot in cold water. Add this to the soup and stir in while continuing to heat another 5 minutes.

9. Taste. Season with mace, salt, and pepper to taste.

10. Add hard cider (apple jack) last. Serve in large shallow soup bowls.

The expression "easy as duck soup" implies richness and the ease that comes with riches. This soup is extravagant in ingredients but turns out not half as rich as some cream soups and makes an elegant light supper for guests. Use only fine Burgundy and try to make the soup when apple cider is in season. The store variety of cider is a poor substitute for the old barn—windfall type.

Burgundy

Orange–Almond Bread

Makes 1 loaf

24 whole almonds
1 large navel orange
1/3 C milk
1/3 C orange juice
2 T honey
1/2 t salt
2 T sweet butter
2 T grated orange rind (fresh)
1 large egg, slightly beaten

1 T yeast
2 C unbleached all-purpose flour
6 orange sections

GLAZE:
1/4 C orange juice
3 T sugar
1/2 T grated orange rind (fresh)
1 T kirsch

1. Blanch, peel, and split almonds. Toast them in oven. Reserve 8 halves. Pulverize the rest in a blender or food processor.

2. Grate orange rind. Peel orange, separate sections, remove pulp.

3. Heat milk and orange juice together. Dissolve honey, salt, butter in milk mixture. Add orange rind, egg, and ground almonds. Cool to warm temperature.

4. When mixture is warm, add and dissolve yeast.

5. Stir in flour and beat well.

6. Spoon 1/3 of dough into well-buttered bread pan, covering the bottom. Place orange slices in 2 rows of 3 sections each, parallel to length of pan. Spread rest of dough over the oranges and smooth. Cover with a cloth and let rise until dough reaches top of pan (1 hour).

7. Pat water on surface of loaf and lightly press on almond halves.

8. Bake at 350 degrees for 25–30 minutes or until richly browned. Remove to wire rack.

9. Mix glaze ingredients together and simmer for at least 10 minutes. Brush on warm loaf.

The glaze, lightly toasted almond halves, and the dark brown top make this a handsome loaf. When the bread is sliced, fresh oranges are revealed. The grated orange rind and toasted almonds nip up the taste. This bread is moist and soft, a good keeper for breakfast.

Assorted fresh fruits

Fish Chowder

2 thick slices of lean bacon, diced
¹/₂ C diced onion
2 sprigs parsley, de-stemmed and minced
1 C peeled and diced potatoes
4 C cold water
salt and pepper

1 lb. white fish fillets
(haddock, flounder, scrod, etc.)
1 small can (5.3 oz.) evaporated milk,
or 1 C light cream

Garnish: *parsley sprigs*

1. Sauté bacon, onion, and parsley in large kettle over medium heat until bacon is browned.

2. Add potatoes, water, salt, and freshly ground pepper to taste.

3. Boil slowly covered 15 minutes.

4. Reduce to a simmer and uncover.

5. Add fish and evaporated milk (or light cream).

6. Simmer 5 minutes more. Do not boil.

7. Break up fish into smaller pieces before serving.

This chowder is mild and filling and a snap to prepare. Any fish fillets may be used, fresh or frozen. Once on the coast of Mexico, we prepared it with the only fish that didn't get away— blowfish. It was the best ever. To complement this easy-going fish chowder, rub your salad bowl with garlic and make up a crunchy coleslaw with olive oil, herb vinegar, and celery seed dressing.

Chenin blanc

Apple Corn Muffins

Makes 8–10

1 C peeled and diced cooking apples
1 C fine yellow cornmeal
1 C unbleached all-purpose flour
¹/₂ t salt
2¹/₂ t baking powder
¹/₂ t baking soda

1 egg, slightly beaten
2 T honey
2 T melted sweet butter
1 C milk

1. Dice apple. Set aside.

2. Sift together cornmeal, flour, salt, baking powder, baking soda.

3. Mix egg, honey, cooled melted butter, and milk.

4. Quickly combine liquid and dry ingredients.

5. Stir in apple.

6. Fill oiled muffin tins half full.

7. Bake 15–20 minutes at 400 degrees or until golden.

The baking soda will begin its leavening action when combined with the honey, so work fast spooning the batter into the tins. A good cooking apple, such as Northern Spy, gives dry corn muffins a refreshing moist taste and texture. Served hot with butter, they'll win over any corn-muffin hater.

Cream cheese

French Onion Soup

2 very large onions
4 T sweet butter
5 t beef extract
5 C water
¹/₄ C dry red wine
¹/₂ C cream

1 crusty baguette sliced into 1-inch thick
pieces left standing a day

Garnish: ¹/₂ C grated Parmesan or
Romano cheese

1. Slice onions into ¹/₄-inch thick slices, cutting parallel to the top.

2. Melt butter in an 8 or 10-inch iron skillet or ovenproof casserole.

3. Simmer onions covered in butter 5–7 minutes, until soft.

4. Stir in beef extract and add water.

5. Bring liquid to a boil. Reduce heat and boil slowly, covered, for 25 minutes.

6. Add wine. While the soup simmers another 5 minutes, toast bread slices on both sides under the broiler.

7. Take the skillet off the burner and let sit 2–3 minutes. Stir in cream.

8. Float toasted French bread on top of the soup and sprinkle generously with Parmesan cheese. Reserve a little cheese to serve in a small dish at the table.

9. Place the soup under broiler until the top is sizzling (approximately 2 minutes).

When Les Halles, the central market, still operated in Paris, the "thing to do" was to stay up all night just to savor a bowl of the French onion soup that truckers and unloaders ate standing up at corner cafés. This author's insomnious night at Les Halles left the memory of a watery tepid soup with very soggy croutons. In this version, the toasted day-old bread rounds stay crisp on top, and the cream is a secret ingredient that adds a rich smooth flavor to the onion broth. From the casserole or skillet on the table, ladle soup into individual gratin bowls, continental style. Follow it by a tossed salad with mustard–oil–vinegar dressing and a cheese–fruit dessert tray.

Médoc

Crusty Baguette

Makes 2

½ C warm water
1 T yeast
1 t salt
½ C water

2 C unbleached all-purpose flour
fine yellow cornmeal
1 egg white
1 T water

1. Dissolve yeast in ½ C warm water in bread bowl.

2. Add salt and ½ C water.

3. Stir in 1 C flour. Beat 200 strokes.

4. Mix in the other cup of flour.

5. Knead 10 minutes. Add extra flour as needed to eliminate sticky dough.

6. Place dough in oiled bowl and let rise until doubled in bulk (1½–2 hours).

7. Punch down, remove from bowl, divide into 2 equal parts.

8. Roll each part into a rectangle less than ½ inch in thickness. With fingers roll dough lengthwise into very tight loaf. Pinch and tuck in ends toward the seam straight across bottom. Pinch seam and loaf-body together.

9. Place seam side down on large oiled baking sheet sprinkled with fine yellow cornmeal. Cover loaves with damp cloth and let rise until doubled in bulk (½–1 hour).

10. With razor blade slit top of each loaf in thirds with diagonal ¾-inch deep slashes.

11. Brush loaves with mixture of 1 egg white and 1 T water. On lower oven shelf place large shallow pan of boiling water.

12. Bake at 400 degrees for 25–30 minutes.

13. Five minutes before they're done, brush tops with water. Cool on wire rack.

Baguette *in French means a rod, wand, or stick. These loaves are rather fat sticks. A French baguette that is extra long and thin is called a flute.*

Rolling the loaves tightly maintains gluten tension to keep the loaf round. Otherwise, it will tend to flatten. The egg wash and the steam from the boiling water produce a rich golden crust. This bread is best served warm—crackling crusty on the outside, sponge soft inside.

Romaine salad

Fruit Soup (Cold)

Serves 6–8

¹/₂ C raisins
¹/₂ C prunes, cooked, pitted,
  and chopped
¹/₂ C dried apricots, chopped
1 C dry red wine
2 C cold water
1 lb. can tart pitted cherries
  with juice
2 tart cooking apples, peeled and diced
1 cinnamon stick

¹/₃ C sugar
¹/₂ t grated orange or lemon rind
4 t arrowroot (2 T corn starch
  may be substituted)
¹/₂ C cold water
sugar to taste

Garnish: ¹/₂ C heavy cream, whipped
  with 1 t confectioners' sugar

1. Soak dried fruit in red wine and water for 1 hour.

2. Place all fruit in large heavy sauce pan with the liquid.

3. Add cinnamon stick and sugar and boil 15 minutes (or until apples are soft but not mushy).

4. Mix arrowroot with ¹/₂ C cold water and add this mixture to soup.

5. If soup is too tart, add more sugar. Add grated orange or lemon rind.

6. Cook soup 2 minutes at slow boil.

7. Chill soup thoroughly. (May be put in freezer compartment until chilled to speed up process.)

8. Serve in chilled glass bowls or compotes with dollops of whipped cream and a sprinkle of nutmeg, cinnamon, and grated orange or lemon rind.

Once this soup maker was invited to a workshop in the Hartz Mountains in Germany where several Danish students decided to take over the kitchen. They produced a fruit soup with a name that sounded like a disease but tasted like ambrosia. They used more thickening agent, however, than this recipe calls for. Since arrowroot is less conspicuous than corn starch, less is needed. The fruits in this recipe are not blended, because one of the delights of this soup is its variety of textures. Served ice cold on a summer day under a shade tree, fruit soup is totally refreshing. It may also be served in smaller portions and without whipped cream as an appetizer.

Rosé

Cinnamon Rolls

Makes 1 dozen

1 C hot milk
1/4 C sweet butter
3 T honey
1 t salt
1 T yeast
1/4 C warm water
1 large egg, slightly beaten
1/2 C mashed potato (medium-size potato)
3 1/2 C unbleached all-purpose flour

FILLING:
3 T melted sweet butter
2 T cinnamon
1/4 C dark brown sugar
1/2 C raisins

TOPPING:
3/4 C confectioners' sugar
2–3 t water
1/8 t almond extract

1. In bread bowl pour hot milk over butter, honey, and salt. Stir to dissolve.

2. In separate small bowl dissolve yeast in water. Add egg to cooled yeast water.

3. Add yeast mixture to lukewarm milk mixture. Beat in potato and 3 C flour.

4. Scrape sides of bowl, cover dough, let rise 2 hours.

5. Stir down. Mix in up to 1/2 C flour. Refrigerate 1 hour.

6. Roll out to 9 × 12-inch rectangle. Brush on melted butter. Sprinkle on brown sugar and cinnamon, mixed together, and raisins. Reserve 1/8 C brown sugar filling.

7. Roll up lengthwise and cut in 1-inch pieces. Place loosely on baking sheet. Cover and let rise 45 minutes. Sprinkle tops with remaining brown sugar–cinnamon mixture.

8. Bake 15–20 minutes at 350 degrees.

9. Mix topping ingredients to pourable consistency. When rolls are slightly cooled, brush on topping.

The mashed potato adds a substantial texture that enhances the hearty flavor of baked dough. These are heavier rolls than the standard cinnamon, but they're equally good tasting. They may also be baked in two 8-inch cake pans.

Gourmandise cheese

Garlic Soup

3 T olive oil
1 C cubed French bread (crouton size)
  left standing 1–2 hours
2 large cloves garlic
1 t paprika
⅛ t cayenne

5 C stock (half chicken, half beef)
2 eggs, slightly beaten
2 T minced parsley
salt to taste

Garnish: *croutons*

1. Heat olive oil in iron frying pan over medium-high heat.

2. Add croutons and brown in oil. When almost brown, press garlic with side of knife, mince, and add to pan.

3. Sauté garlic and croutons approximately 3 more minutes.

4. Take out ¾ of croutons and reserve.

5. Add paprika, cayenne, and stock to those croutons left in pan.

6. Bring soup to a fast boil.

7. Remove pan from heat and then quickly add eggs, parsley, and salt while stirring.

8. Cover and let stand 5 minutes.

9. Warm bowls with hot water. Serve a few saturated croutons in each bowl and let guests help themselves to the crisp croutons at the table.

Some people do not mind soggy croutons. In fact, the French often blend soaked bread (panades) into their soups as a thickening agent. We prefer leaving out most of the croutons and serving them crisp at the table. If you don't tell your guests this is garlic soup, they'll never know. It's not one of those famous recipes that starts out, "Take 16 large cloves of garlic . . . ." Garlic soup, French bread, a fine French wine and cheese make a well-rounded meal. In fact, "Fantastique!"

Claret

Crusty Rolls

1 T yeast
1/4 C warm water
1 1/2 t salt
1 T corn oil
3/4 C water

1 egg white
3 1/2 C unbleached all-purpose flour
fine yellow cornmeal
1 egg yolk
1 T water

1. Dissolve yeast in 1/4 C warm water.

2. Add salt, oil, 3/4 C water, and egg white.

3. Stir in 2 C flour and beat 200 strokes.

4. Mix in 1 C flour.

5. Knead 10 minutes on board, adding 1/2 C flour as needed to prevent sticking.

6. Cover and let rise in oiled bowl until doubled in bulk (1–1 1/2 hours).

7. Punch down. Remove from bowl. Cut into 16 equal parts.

8. Round each part by continuously folding underneath and into center of roll to form smooth-topped ball.

9. Place rolls on lightly oiled baking sheet sprinkled with cornmeal. Cover and let rise until nearly doubled in bulk (1 hour).

10. Mix egg yolk and water. Brush tops with egg yolk wash. With kitchen scissors cut tops with 1-inch deep X.

11. Place shallow pan of boiling water on lower shelf of oven. Bake rolls 12–15 minutes at 375 degrees or until golden.

These rolls are dense, thick-crusted, and chewy. Since the dough is folded into itself several times, the roll will maintain a tension and round shape during baking. The X cut in the top makes the roll blossom open in the oven. Brush the rolls with the French egg wash to deepen their color.

Brie cheese

Gazpacho (Cold)

Serves 4

2 C diced peeled fresh ripe tomatoes
1 C seeded, diced green pepper
1 C peeled, seeded, and diced cucumber
1 clove garlic, minced
1/8 C diced Bermuda onion
2 T olive oil
3 T lemon juice
1 1/2 C tomato–vegetable juice

1/8 t cayenne
salt to taste
2 T bread crumbs

Garnish: 1 t fresh de-stemmed minced parsley,
1 t fresh minced chives, and any
other herbs. Add water to make
herb ice cubes. Freeze.

1. Prepare all vegetables (peel, seed, dice).

2. Mix vegetables together. Put half into a blender or food processor and purée (not too fine).

3. Repeat with remaining vegetables.

4. Place puréed vegetables in a large bowl. Stir in olive oil, lemon juice, tomato–vegetable juice, cayenne and salt.

5. Stir in bread crumbs.

6. Chill the soup 2 hours or more. The soup will chill quicker if ingredients are cold before preparation.

7. Place an herb ice cube in each bowl.

Gazpacho takes only a few minutes to prepare and tastes as fresh as your garden on a summer day.

Portuguese rosé

Triticale Muffins

1³/₄ C triticale flour
2 t baking powder
¹/₂ t salt
²/₃ C cooked hominy grits
³/₄ C milk

1 egg, slightly beaten
2 T melted sweet butter
2 T blackstrap molasses
¹/₄ C strong black coffee,
    freshly brewed

1. Mix flour, baking powder, salt.

2. Combine cooled grits, milk, egg, cooled butter, molasses, and cooled coffee in separate bowl.

3. Pour the grits mixture into the flour mixture and stir well.

4. Spoon into oiled muffin tins. Bake 20 minutes at 400 degrees, or until crusty on top. Serve hot with sweet butter.

Triticale is a hybrid grain of wheat and rye. Besides offering a greater usable yield than either wheat or rye, triticale contains significantly more—and higher quality—protein. With the increasing public awareness of nutrition, triticale will eventually make its way to the supermarket shelf. Right now you may find it in most health food stores. Its nut-like flavor is subtle but apparent. These muffins are substantial and walnut-brown. The grits help keep them moist longer.

Goat's milk cheese

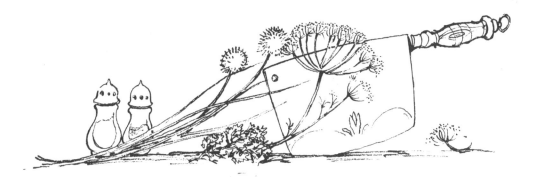

Leek Soup

4 leeks, white part only, sliced thin
  (approximately 1 fully packed C)
1/4 C chopped onion
2 T sweet butter
2 C diced potatoes
2 C chicken stock

1 1/2 C half and half
1/8 t mace
1 t chervil
salt and white pepper to taste

Garnish: *minced chives*

1. Sauté leeks and onions in butter until soft.

2. Add potatoes and stock.

3. Simmer covered for 15 minutes.

4. Work vegetables and stock through a food mill using the medium fine disc, or blend until fine but not puréed.

5. Return mixture to pot and add half and half.

6. Season with mace, chervil, salt and pepper.

7. Reheat until hot. Do not boil.

8. Serve piping hot or ice cold.

The leek is to the Welsh what laurel was to the Romans. Heroic Welsh soldiers wore it in their helmets and adopted it as their emblem. In the United States this stalwart member of the onion family is sadly neglected. In the summer leek–potato soup served chilled is known as Vichyssoise.

Dry white Mousseux or brut Champagne

Yam Rolls

1 ¹/₂ C boiled and mashed yams
   (2 medium-size yams)
3 T sweet butter
1 T yeast
1 C warm water from boiled yams

¹/₂ t salt
1 egg, slightly beaten
3 ¹/₄ C unbleached all-purpose flour

1. Boil and mash yams. Reserve 1 C water.

2. Add butter to hot mashed yams and stir.

3. Dissolve yeast in warm yam water. Add salt, egg, and 2 C flour; beat thoroughly. Add 1 more C flour. Dough will be sticky.

4. Pour into oiled bowl and let rise until doubled in bulk (1 hour).

5. Stir down and add approximately ¹/₄ C flour. Dough will still be thin.

6. Spoon into oiled muffin tins. Let rise until doubled in bulk (¹/₂ hour).

7. Bake at 350 degrees for 12–15 minutes or until lightly browned.

These rolls come out of the oven a delicate apricot color and are appealing with just about any dish. Besides this, they are feather-light and spongy with a very faint taste of yams. When preparing them, you'll think they'll never rise, but if your yeast is active (don't kill it with boiling water) they will blossom.

Camembert cheese

Lentil Lemon Soup

1 1/2 C lentils, washed
6 C water
2 C chicken or beef stock
1 potato (large) cut into
   1-inch pieces
1 lb. Swiss chard (if
   unavailable, spinach)
1/3 C minced onion
3 cloves garlic

4 T olive oil
2 T fresh minced celery leaves
1/4 t coriander
salt and freshly ground pepper
3 T lemon juice
1/2 t cumin
link pork sausages (2 per person)

Garnish: *thin lemon slices*

1. Place lentils, water, and stock in soup pot and bring to a boil. (A soup bone may be added for extra flavor.)

2. Turn heat to medium.

3. Wash and drain chard. Take out the central white stem and slice layers of leaves into thin shreds. (Other greens may be substituted.)

4. Add greens and potatoes. Slowly boil the soup, covered, for 45 minutes.

5. Crush garlic cloves first to enhance flavor, then mince with onion. Add to hot olive oil in a small frying pan. Sauté until tender. Add celery leaves and coriander.

6. Add onion mixture to the soup.

7. Brown sausages while the soup simmers another 5 minutes. (If sausages are not precooked, start them with the onions.)

8. Stir in salt, pepper, lemon juice, and cumin at the last minute.

9. Serve in deep pottery bowls with 2 link sausages cut up into each serving.

Each bowl is an entire meal of meat, potatoes, legumes, and a green vegetable. The lemon juice and cumin are secret ingredients that cut through the heavy lentil taste and levitate the palate.

Ale

Light Dinner Rolls

Makes 16

1 T yeast
¹/₄ C warm water
4 T melted sweet butter
1 t salt
1 T honey

1 C warm water
1 egg, slightly beaten
3 C unbleached all-purpose flour

1. Dissolve yeast in ¹/₄ C water.

2. Melt butter.

3. Dissolve salt and honey in 1 C warm water. Pour in cooled butter.

4. Add yeast and egg.

5. Stir in 2 C flour and beat 200 strokes. Add remaining flour and mix well.

6. Place batter-like dough in large oiled bowl and let rise until doubled in bulk (2 or more hours).

7. Punch down. Shape rolls into rounds and place in oiled tins, filling cups ¹/₃–¹/₂ full.

8. Cover and let rise until doubled in bulk (45 minutes).

9. Bake at 400 degrees for 10–12 minutes.

These are light and spongy and relatively quick to prepare for good yeasted dinner rolls. The dough, or batter, may be gluey to work with (keep your fingers oiled when shaping the rolls), but the result is worth it. They may also be cooked in an 8- or 9-inch lightly oiled cake pan, although their shapes will be less distinct.

Young Gouda

Lobster Bisque

Serves 4

1 boiled lobster (1–1½ lbs.)
1 T dry sherry
1½ C fish stock
1½ C chicken stock
1 small stalk celery with leaves
2 cloves
3 peppercorns
1 small bay leaf, crushed
1 C dry white wine (Bordeaux works well)

3 T sweet butter
1½ T flour
1 C milk
¾ C cream
1 egg yolk, slightly beaten
salt and white pepper to taste

Garnish: *dash of nutmeg*

1. Remove all the lobster meat from tail and claws. Shred it into small pieces. Cover it with sherry and set aside.

2. Crush shells with a mallet or lobster crackers (nut crackers will do) and disjoint the legs, retaining as much of the juices as possible for the lobster stock. The softer leg pieces may be ground in a meat grinder and added to the pot along with the fish stock, chicken stock, celery, cloves, peppercorns, bay leaf, and wine (omit the wine if it is used in your fish stock recipe). Cook all these ingredients at a slow boil, uncovered, for 30 minutes. If fish heads, tails, et cetera, are unavailable for a good fish stock, boil 1 C clam juice, 1 C dry white wine, celery stalk, sprig of parsley, small chopped onion, and 3 peppercorns for 15 minutes and strain.

3. Strain the lobster stock through a double layer of cheesecloth into a bowl.

4. In a medium sauce pan melt butter and make a roux with flour. Slowly add the milk and cook over medium-low heat, stirring constantly. Do not boil.

5. Add 1½ C lobster stock and lobster meat to the milk sauce. Continue cooking over medium heat, stirring constantly.

6. Mix cream well with egg yolk and add it to the bisque, making sure the soup is hot but never boils. Bisque should be the consistency of heavy cream.

7. Season with a dash of nutmeg, salt and pepper to taste. Note: The lobster will be salty, so make sure to taste the bisque first.

This is one soup for which there are few substitutes. The lobster should be fresh and if you can't bring yourself to commit crustacicide, make sure your favorite fish market boiled the lobster red that day. A little of this soup goes a long way. (It's rich and you have to be rich to make it!)

White Bordeaux

74

Sourdough French Bread

1 large loaf

STARTER:
2 C reconstituted dry milk
2 C unbleached all-purpose flour

¹/₂ C warm water
1 T yeast
1 t salt
1 T corn oil
1 C water
4¹/₂ C unbleached all-purpose flour
yellow cornmeal

1. Blend starter ingredients and place in glass or plastic container. Cover with cheesecloth for 2 days and let stand in warm room or until starter turns curdy and sour.

2. Dissolve yeast in warm water. Add salt, oil, and 1 C water.

3. Peel crust from starter and discard. Add starter to yeast mixture. Stir in 2 C flour and beat 200 strokes.

4. Add 2 C more flour. Dough will be very pliable.

5. Knead 10 minutes, adding only enough flour to avoid stickiness.

6. Place in oiled bowl, cover, and let rise until doubled in bulk (1¹/₂ hours).

7. Punch down. Let rest on board 10 minutes. Dough will be soft. Roll out to rectangle ¹/₂ inch thick.

8. Roll loosely by hand from long side. Pinch end edges to body of loaf. Place on large baking sheet, oiled and sprinkled lightly with yellow cornmeal. Cover. Let rise until doubled in bulk (1 hour).

9. With razor blade slash bread with 3 evenly spaced 1-inch deep diagonal cuts. Place in cold oven and turn on heat to 350 degrees. Bake 40–50 minutes or until golden.

A dry milk starter has concentrated lactose and makes a better, stronger starter. You may reduce the sourness of the finished bread by adding ¹/₂ t baking soda, but personally we like the full strength. Since the starter traps free-floating natural yeast, you're at the whim of the wilds. We've found that in our location without the addition of commercial yeast the leavening action is too slow. (The unique San Francisco sourdough can be made only there because of a strain of yeasts peculiar to the Bay area.) Making a starter brings you closer to the essence of breadmaking. This recipe should produce a crusty, chewy, rough-textured, tangy loaf.

Emmenthal cheese

Meat Borscht

2 lbs. chuck beef
water to cover (approximately 4 C)
1 C cooked diced beets
6 C shredded cabbage
1 C shredded carrots
One 6-oz. can tomato paste
⅓ C white vinegar
4 sprigs parsley

6 peppercorns
2 bay leaves
2–4 additional C water
1 t sugar
salt to taste

Garnish: ½ C sour cream

1. Trim fat or gristle from beef and cut meat into bite-size pieces.

2. Cover meat with water.

3. Bring to boil, cover, lower heat, boil slowly.

4. After meat is tender as a maiden's kiss, strain off broth. (Cooking should take at least 1½ hours at a slow boil.)

5. Place all vegetables in a large soup kettle with the meat broth, tomato paste, and vinegar.

6. Make a bouquet garni by tying herbs in a piece of cheesecloth with cotton thread or string. Add the bouquet to soup.

7. Boil the vegetables slowly ½ hour. Then add the meat and cook another ½ hour over low heat, pouring in additional water (2–4 C) when the soup gets too thick.

8. Add sugar and salt to taste.

9. Remove the bouquet garni and ladle borscht into bowls, adding a dollop of sour cream to each.

"The maiden's kiss" came with the original recipe. When the recipe was given to us, it was emphasized that "This is an approximate recipe in conversational style." So don't worry too much about exact measurements. If you have an extra carrot or beet, put it in. The longer the soup simmers and the oftener it is warmed up the better it gets.

German dark beer

Onion Bagels

Makes 14–16

1 T yeast
1 C potato water
1 T corn oil
1 t salt
1 egg, slightly beaten

1 egg white (reserve yolk)
¹/₂ C dried onion flakes
3¹/₂–4 C unbleached all-purpose flour
2 T honey

1. Dissolve yeast in warm potato water.

2. Add oil, salt, whole egg, egg white, and 5 T onion flakes.

3. Gradually stir in 3¼ C flour.

4. Knead 15 minutes, adding extra flour as needed.

5. Break off tennis-ball-size pieces of dough and roll each between your palms into ropes 7 inches long, ³/₄ inch thick. Wet ends and pinch together to form circles. Place on lightly oiled baking sheet.

6. Cover and let rise until doubled in bulk.

7. To 2 quarts of boiling water add 2 T honey. Drop bagels one at a time into water (no more than 2 or 3 in the pot at once) for approximately 3 minutes. They will expand and float.

8. Remove with slotted spoon and dry on wire rack.

9. Add 1 T water to reserved egg yolk. Brush wash on bagels and press on remaining 3 T onion flakes. Place bagels on lightly oiled or aluminum foiled baking sheet.

10. Bake at 325 degrees for 20 minutes or until richly golden.

These boiled and baked donut-like rolls reach their height with cream cheese and smoked salmon. They may be made with fresh sautéed onions, or with sesame or poppy seeds sprinkled on, or just plain and delicious. When we first began making bagels, they shriveled up like blistered paint. This recipe avoids that problem.

Cream cheese

Minestrone alla Fiori

Serves 6–7

1 beef bone
8 C cold water
1/3 C dry beans (white or pink),
  soaked 4–5 hours (or overnight),
  and drained
2 C whole peeled tomatoes
3 cloves garlic
8–10 sprigs fresh parsley,
  washed and de-stemmed
5–6 sprigs fresh basil, washed
  and de-stemmed
3 T olive oil

2 T grated Parmesan or Romano
  cheese
2 carrots, pared and diced
2 medium-size potatoes, peeled
  and quartered
2 C washed, shredded,
  fresh spinach or other greens
salt to taste
1 C uncooked pasta

Garnish: grated Parmesan or
  Romano cheese

1. Place bone in soup pot. Add water.

2. Bring to a boil, skimming scum when necessary.

3. Add beans and tomatoes. Cover and boil slowly 1/2 hour.

4. Meanwhile, crush peeled garlic cloves and mince with fresh parsley and basil, using a *mezza luna* or other sharp chopping tool. This mixture is a *pesto* base.

5. Place *pesto* in a mortar or small heavy bowl and blend in olive oil and 2 T grated Parmesan cheese. Let stand covered at room temperature.

6. After tomatoes and beans have cooked 1/2 hour, add other vegetables to soup.

7. Boil slowly, covered, for another 1/2 hour (or until potatoes are soft).

8. Remove pieces of potato with a slotted spoon. Place potatoes in a shallow bowl and mash them well into a cup of the liquid.

9. Add mashed potatoes to the soup pot along with the *pesto*.

10. Salt to taste.

11. Reheat minestrone to a boil and add 1 C dried pasta. (Vermicelli broken into small pieces, small bows, thin macaroni, or any other type of pasta may be used.)

12. Boil with lid slightly ajar. Pasta should be *al dente*.

Minestrone is always served with a bowl of Parmesan on the table. A spunky Northern Italian, Nilda Fiori taught one of us the basics of Northern Italian peasant cooking. Whether Nilda was making veal scaloppine, osso buco (veal shanks), or spaghetti Bolognese, her first step was to mix a pesto of garlic, parsley, basil, olive oil, and Parmesan cheese. When minced finely and blended well, these ingredients form a marriage. Minestrone is the Italian's vegetable scrap soup. No two minestrones are alike. Let the pesto be the common ingredient and invent your own variations.

Chianti

Bread Sticks

Makes 50 or more

1 T yeast
¹/₄ C warm water
1 C water
1 t salt
1 T olive oil
1 garlic clove, minced

1 egg white
3¹/₄–3¹/₂ C unbleached
  all-purpose flour
1 egg yolk
1 T water
salt and favorite seasoning
  (sesame seeds, thyme, rosemary, etc.)

1. Dissolve yeast in ¹/₄ C water in bread bowl.

2. Stir in 1 C water, salt, oil, garlic, egg white.

3. Add 2 C flour. Beat 200 strokes. Add 1 C flour.

4. Knead 5 minutes, adding ¼–½ C flour as needed. Cover and let rise until doubled in bulk (1¹/₂ hours).

5. Punch down. Stretch out on board. Break off pieces the size of a walnut. Roll them as thin and evenly as possible between your palms — about 5–6 inches long, ¹/₄ inch thick.

6. Place sticks on ungreased baking sheet. Mix egg yolk and water. With fingers coat sticks with egg yolk wash. Sprinkle on salt and then any one or a combination of seasonings.

7. Bake immediately for about 20 minutes at 300 degrees.

Coarse salt is a good coating, but if you don't have any handy, standard table salt works, too. Salt and thyme are especially good. Bread sticks with a variety of seeds and herbs add zip to a meal. When shaping the sticks, make them pencil thin. If they're too thick, they won't crisp. The egg yolk wash provides the adhesive for the seasonings, and a darker color. Bread sticks take time to fix. You may reduce the overall time by baking one batch while preparing the next. Serve them in a tall glass.

Provolone cheese

Minted Pea Soup (Cold)

Serves 4

2 C chicken stock
1 C water
¼ C mint (3 large sprigs)
3 C peas (not canned!)
½ C diced onion

½ C heavy cream
salt to taste

Garnish: *whipped cream
and fresh mint leaves*

1. Bring chicken stock, water, and mint to a boil.

2. Drop peas and onions into rapidly boiling stock.

3. Cover and cook peas at a slow boil until tender (no longer than 12 minutes).

4. Cool and work through a food mill, using the finest disc. (Note: A blender will not do in this case. The outer skins of some peas are tough and won't blend well.)

5. Stir the cream into the purée.

6. Salt to taste.

7. Chill the soup in a pitcher.

8. If the soup separates, simply stir it well before pouring into chilled bowls.

9. Top with whipped cream and a small mint leaf sprig.

Most recipes for green pea soup, either hot or cold, call for sugar, but you'll discover how naturally sweet peas are without this addition. Peas picked straight from the vine yield a fresh tingling soup.

Sauterne

Honey Lime Rolls

Makes 8

2 T melted sweet butter
1 T honey
1/2 C buttermilk
1 T yeast

3/4 t lime extract
1 C unbleached all-purpose flour
1/2 t salt
3 1/2 t baking soda

1. Melt butter and honey in warmed buttermilk. Cool slightly.

2. Dissolve yeast in warm buttermilk mixture. Add lime.

3. Mix together flour, salt, baking soda.

4. Combine flour and buttermilk mixtures.

5. Knead 5 minutes, adding flour as needed to prevent sticking.

6. Divide dough into 8 equal parts. Round each piece into a smooth ball. Place in buttered round 8-inch cake pan. Cover. Let rise until doubled in bulk (45 minutes).

7. Bake at 375 degrees for 8–10 minutes or until lightly browned. (If browned too soon, cover with aluminum foil for rest of baking.)

As they're baking the whiff of lime is a sun-drenched summer smell. The interior of these soft rolls is amber-colored, the texture very light. Perfect for the minted pea soup suggested here.

Gourmandise cheese

Molded Chinese Soup

Serves 4

1 large chicken breast, split
1 dried Chinese mushroom
  (soaked in ¹/₂ C water)
6 oz. cooked thin ham, sliced
  in ¹/₄-inch wide strips
4 oz. sliced water chestnuts

3 slices ginger root
  (¹/₄-inch thick)
2 green onions (stems and all)
  cut into 1-inch pieces
sesame or peanut oil
2 eggs, slightly beaten

8–10 whole snow peas
4¹/₂ C chicken stock
soy sauce to taste

Garnish: alfalfa sprouts

1. Steam chicken breast in a steamer 7–10 minutes.

2. Tear meat off chicken into shreds.

3. Soak dried mushroom in warm water and remove stem. Rinse. Drain.

4. Prepare ham, water chestnuts, ginger, green onions. Refrigerate all meats and vegetables until ready for use.

5. In an 8-inch frying pan coated with oil, make 2 very thin omelets one at a time. Slice into long ¹/₂ inch strips.

6. In bowl with a bottom at least 6–8 inches in diameter, center mushroom, smooth side down. Arrange chicken, ham, and egg strips alternately spiraling from sides of mushroom. (Ingredients may be layered up sides of bowl, too). Fill in with snow peas and green onions. Place water chestnut strips at center of wheel.

7. Press ingredients down tightly with palm of your hand or a spatula. Cover them with ¹/₂ C stock and sprinkle with soy sauce.

8. Place bowl in steamer, or large covered wok. Fill steamer bottom with approximately 2 inches of water and place bowl of vegetables and meats on a trivet in the bottom. Cover. Steam 20 minutes.

9. In a separate pan heat chicken stock to slow boil. Select a serving bowl that will hold the steamed vegetable bowl, or use your wok.

10. Invert steamed vegetable bowl in the bottom of the serving bowl (as you would to turn out an upside-down cake). But don't remove the bowl-mold. Instead, pour the stock around the inverted bowl. The suction of the liquid around the mold will release any vegetables that might stick to the bottom of the mold.

11. Now, pry up the molded vegetable bowl with 2 spoons and carefully lift it off. The Chinese vegetables and meats will float in a circular molded shape in the stock.

12. Serve immediately at the table from the large serving bowl.

When we first heard of this concept adapted from **Pei Mei's Chinese Cookbook,** *it wasn't clear what was happening. We couldn't understand why you would pour stock over an inverted bowl and exactly how this Chinese flower would stay together. To understand, you must try it.*

Many substitutes may be made for the vegetables and meats—bamboo shoots instead of water chestnuts, lobster or shrimp for the chicken. Keep color and design in mind. Chinese molded soup sounds fancy but is simple and exciting to prepare.

Lapsang Souchong tea

Cha Siew Bao
(Steamed buns filled with pork)

Makes 10–12

BUNS:
1 T yeast
$^1/_2$ C warm water
$^1/_4$ t salt
1 C unbleached all-purpose
   flour

FILLING:
$^1/_2$ lb. ground mild pork
   sausage (or ground pork)
3 scallions, minced
$^1/_2$ t fresh ginger,
   grated
peanut oil

1. Dissolve yeast in water. Stir in salt. Mix in flour.

2. Knead 5 minutes or until smooth and elastic.

3. Cover. Let rise 1 hour.

4. Sauté scallions and ginger in peanut oil.

5. Add meat and brown well. Mash up into small pieces. Set aside.

6. Punch down dough. Break off small egg-size pieces and pat flat into 3-inch circles.

7. Place a tablespoon of pork mixture in center of each circle. Bring two opposite edges over and seal. With a knife cut off excess dough from remaining sides, leaving enough to seal in pork. Gently seal sides, tuck under along seam, and form miniature loaves.

8. Cover and let rise for 15–20 minutes.

9. Over boiling water place buns well apart in steamer basket to allow for expansion. Cover with lid. Steam for 5–10 minutes or until surface glistens and is firm to the touch. Serve warm.

These make simple, intriguing appetizers. Once you get the knack, they're relatively easy and quick to prepare. The unusual effect of steaming the buns offers a novel change of texture and taste. Any kind of meat or vegetable filling may be used.

Tofu

Mulligatawny Soup

Serves 6

3 slices salt pork, diced
(4 inches long, ¹/₄ inch thick)
1³/₄–2 lbs. chicken cut into
small frying pieces as for
fricassee
¹/₂ C diced green pepper
¹/₃ C diced carrot
¹/₃ C diced onion
1 T flour
1¹/₂ t curry

3 peppercorns
2 cloves
1 small bay leaf
8 C water
1 C tomato pulp
¹/₂ t cayenne
salt to taste

Garnish: steamed white rice, and cream
of coconut or coconut milk

1. Fry salt pork and remove the lardoons (pork pieces).

2. In a heavy frying pan fry chicken in the pork fat over medium-high heat.

3. Add diced vegetables and fry for 5 minutes with chicken.

4. Transfer contents to a large soup pot.

5. Mix flour and curry powder. Sprinkle evenly over chicken and vegetables.

6. With the back of a knife crush peppercorns. Add to the chicken with the cloves and bay leaf.

7. Cook over high heat for 2 minutes, then add the water and bring to a boil.

8. Boil the soup slowly 1¹/₂ hours.

9. The last half-hour, add tomato pulp.

10. Remove chicken pieces, cloves, and bay leaf. Work the vegetables and broth through a strainer or fine disc of a food mill.

11. Return the purée to the pot. Add cayenne. Salt to taste.

12. Bring to a boil. Meanwhile, discard chicken bones and skin and shred the chicken meat into bite-size pieces.

13. Add chicken to the mulligatawny. Serve very hot with a bowl of fluffy white rice.

Mulligatawny is a south Indian word which literally means "pepper water," so the spicier the soup the better. Since even peppercorns will lose their potency after a year in the cupboard, the spices should be as fresh as possible. Cream of coconut is a purée similar in texture to fudge sauce. Half a teaspoon melted in each bowl lends an exotic flavor to this soup.

Darjeeling tea

Fan Tan Rolls

Makes 2½ dozen

1 T yeast
1 C warm milk
2 T melted sweet butter
¾ t salt (scant)

1 egg, slightly beaten
2¾ C unbleached all-purpose
  flour
5 T melted sweet butter

1. Dissolve yeast in milk.

2. Add 2 T butter, salt, egg.

3. Add 2 C flour and beat 200 strokes. Mix in ½ C more flour.

4. Place in oiled bowl, cover, and let rise until doubled in bulk (1–1½ hours).

5. Punch down. Knead a few minutes, adding no more than ¼ C extra flour.

6. Roll ⅛ inch thick to approximately 20 × 10-inch rectangle. Trim edges into straight sides. Brush 3 T melted butter on top.

7. From width cut 10 long strips 1 inch wide. Cut strips into 1-inch segments (200 in all).

8. Stack 6 segments loosely and place each stack up-ended in a shallow muffin tin.

9. Let rise until doubled in bulk (½ hour). Pour on remaining melted butter.

10. Bake 15 minutes at 425 degrees or until lightly golden.

A mezza luna makes a good dough cutter for these. When preparing fan tans, try to be as exact as possible in cutting the segments so that the end result will be a uniform set of "leaves" of light, airy, buttery bread that unfolds like a fan.

Ambrosia salad

Mushroom Soup

Serves 4

3 C peeled sliced mushrooms
3 T sweet butter
4 t minced shallots
1/8 t thyme
1 t minced fresh parsley
1/8 t ground rosemary

3 T dry sherry
2 T flour
2 1/2 C beef broth
1 egg yolk
1 C light cream
dash of nutmeg

Garnish: *whipped cream*

1. Peel mushrooms and remove woody part of stems. Slice in crescents. (Approximately 1 lb. mushrooms yields 3 C.)

2. In sauce pan over medium heat sauté mushrooms, shallots, and herbs in melted butter until mushrooms go limp.

3. Add sherry and cook covered 5 more minutes.

4. Remove pan from heat. Add flour and stir well.

5. Slowly add beef broth, stirring constantly.

6. Return pan to low heat and bring liquid to slow boil.

7. In separate bowl beat egg yolk, cream, and nutmeg together with a whisk.

8. Again remove pan from heat. Slowly add the cream mixture, stirring constantly.

9. Blend 1 C of the soup (making sure to include approximately 1/2 C mushrooms) at low speed or pass through the fine disc of a food mill.

10. Return blended cup of soup to pan and reheat contents, but do not boil.

11. Scoop a mound of freshly whipped cream onto each serving.

In this recipe, the egg yolk and blended mushrooms thicken the soup. Yet, delicate morsels of mushrooms are still afloat to titillate the palate that loves texture. Peeling mushrooms is a trick learned from a friend. Washed mushrooms don't sauté as well as peeled because of the added moisture. If snow-white firm mushroom caps are unavailable in your local store and a special occasion calls for a choice soup, use the grocer's bargain table mushrooms. You will find that the mushroom when peeled is still quite white and firm underneath.

White Burgundy

Petites Brioches

1 T yeast
1/4 C warm water
2 eggs, slightly beaten
1 egg white
2 C unbleached all-purpose flour

1 t salt
1/2 t grated lemon rind
1/4 lb. sweet butter
1 egg yolk
1 T water

1. Dissolve yeast in warm water. Add 2 eggs plus 1 egg white.

2. Mix flour, salt, and lemon rind.

3. Add yeast mixture to flour mixture. Knead by continually throwing sticky elastic dough into bowl for 5–10 minutes.

4. Work small pieces of butter into dough.

5. Cover and refrigerate at least 1 hour.

6. Knead briefly and quickly on board. Reserve a quarter of the dough for topknots. Working without delay, form rolls by breaking off large egg-size pieces and placing them in ungreased fluted or muffin tins.

7. With scissors cut a deep X in the center of each roll. To make topknot, roll a walnut-size piece of dough into cone shape. Gently insert point into exact center of X cut. Tuck in snugly. Repeat with each roll.

8. Cover and let rise slightly for 1/2–1 hour. Mix egg yolk and water. With fingers gently coat brioches with French egg yolk wash.

9. Bake 10–12 minutes at 450 degrees.

Petites brioches are small, festive-looking, top-hatted French rolls. They're an irresistible concoction of buttery layers of dough combined with rich sturdiness. They're most attractive baked in special fluted brioche tins, but standard muffin cups work as well. This is a bread to get your hands in. Dig the butter into the dough and then throw it around to develop the gluten. When cool the butter hardens and gives the impression the brioches are old, so serve them warm.

Havarti cheese

Mustard Soup

2 T sweet butter
2 T flour
2¹/₂ C chicken broth
1 C light cream or half and
   half
¹/₂ C milk
salt and white pepper to taste

¹/₂ t onion juice
2 egg yolks, beaten
3 T light cream or half and
   half
3 T prepared mustard

Garnish: *paprika*

1. Melt butter and make a roux with flour in a heavy sauce pan.

2. Add chicken broth, cream, milk.

3. Add salt and white pepper to taste. Add onion juice.

4. Simmer over low heat 10 minutes until milk is scalded. Do not boil.

5. In separate bowl beat egg yolks and 3 T cream until smooth.

6. Slowly add approximately 1 C of the hot soup mixture to egg mixture, whisking constantly.

7. Pour this liaison into the pan with the rest of the soup, whisking constantly.

8. Reheat. Stir all the time for a smooth consistency. Never boil.

9. Add mustard last, stirring it in.

10. Serve soup in small portions. Sprinkle with paprika.

This recipe for mustard soup is a variation of a 14th century receipt from Le Viandier *compiled by Guillaume Tirel for Charles V's kitchen staff.*

Mustard soup is not served with hot dogs. It has a delicate flavor and smooth rich texture that make it a wonderful first course for baked ham or a standing rib roast. Choose your favorite prepared mustard. The flavor permeates throughout the soup and will not be too strong.

Burgundy

Dill Bread

Makes 1 loaf

1 T yeast
1/4 C warm water
1 T honey
1 T corn oil
1 t salt
1 large egg, slightly beaten
1/2 C cottage cheese

1/2 C yogurt
1 T minced onion
1/4 t baking soda
1 T dill seed
1 t dill leaf
1 C whole wheat flour
1 C unbleached all-purpose flour

1. Dissolve yeast in warm water.

2. Add all the rest of the ingredients in the order listed.

3. Stir and mix well for 1–2 minutes.

4. Cover and let rise until doubled in bulk (2 or more hours).

5. Punch or stir down. Place in oiled 1 1/2-quart oval ovenproof bowl.

6. Bake 30 minutes at 350 degrees.

Batter breads such as this are easy to make. This one produces a moist, very spongy texture, and a modest dill flavor. Dill stimulates the taste buds. You may increase the dill taste by adding a teaspoon more of both seed and leaf. Bake the bread in an oval bowl. The bread will turn out with a walnut-colored crust and attractive shape.

Tilsit cheese

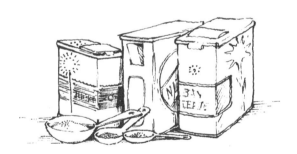

Navy Bean Soup

1 C navy beans (soaked
  at least 5 hours)
7 C hot water
1 C tomato juice
  (or vegetable-tomato juice)
1 smoked ham hock
1 bay leaf
¾ C diced onion
½ C diced carrots
½ C chopped celery and leaves

1 clove garlic, minced
½ C milk
1 C cooked diced potatoes
1 t sweet butter
salt and freshly ground white pepper
  to taste
2 t white vinegar
1 pinch crushed red pepper

Garnish: minced chives

1. Drain and wash soaked beans. Discard any floating beans or skins.

2. Place beans in large soup pot and cover them with water and tomato juice.

3. Over medium-high heat bring to boil. Add the ham hock, bay leaf, onion, carrots, celery, and garlic.

4. Reduce heat. Cover and boil slowly until the beans are tender. (Start sampling after an hour.) The beans must be soft, but not cooked so long that the skins fall off.

5. Remove bay leaf and ham hock.

6. Place milk, cooked diced potatoes, and butter in a blender. Purée.

7. Strain soup vegetables, reserving the liquid.

8. Place 2 heaping cups of beans and vegetables plus 2 C of liquid in the blender with potatoes.

9. Purée contents of blender and return to soup pot. Add remaining whole beans and liquid to soup.

10. Salt and pepper to taste. Add vinegar and crushed red pepper at your discretion.

Navy beans are not always called "navy" beans on the package. They are a small white bean which New Englanders often use for the baked bean pot. Follow the directions on the package for presoaking. Some beans have been treated so that soaking is unnecessary. If no directions appear on the package, soak anyway. It will reduce the cooking time. Using the smoked ham hock, rather than salt pork or pork hock, imparts a much more distinctive flavor to this soup.

Cold milk

Boston Brown Bread

Makes 2 loaves

1 C raisins
1/2 C rum
1 C fine yellow cornmeal
1 C rye flour
1 C whole wheat flour
1 t baking soda

1 t baking powder
1 t salt
2 C buttermilk
1 C blackstrap molasses
2 T corn oil
1/2 C freshly brewed black coffee

1. Soak raisins in rum for 6 hours or more.

2. Mix cornmeal, rye and whole wheat flours, baking soda, baking powder, salt.

3. In separate bowl mix buttermilk, molasses, oil, coffee.

4. Combine with cornmeal mixture. Add raisins and excess rum.

5. Pour into two buttered 1 lb. coffee cans, filling slightly more than half full. Oil plastic lids. Cap cans with lids (or aluminum foil) and tie tops on like a package.

6. Steam for 1–11/2 hours.

If you don't have a steamer, one alternative is to place a trivet on the bottom of a large kettle. Bring an inch or two of water to a boil and place filled cans on trivet. Cover the kettle. You'll have an easy-to-do, moist, fresh-tasting bread. Check periodically to see if the bread is cooked. When the top of the loaf is firm to the touch through the lid, it's done. One advantage to plastic lids is that you can check the progress without removing the tops. Don't overcook, or the special moistness associated with Boston brown bread will be lost.

Cream cheese

New England Clam Chowder

½ C diced salt pork
1 medium onion, diced
2 C diced potatoes
2 C clam juice (2 dozen
   shucked cherrystones
   yield approximately 2 C.
   Bottled juice may be used.)
1½ C cold water

1 C minced clams (2 dozen
   shucked cherrystones yield
   approximately 1 C. Canned
   minced clams may be used.)
1 C half and half or light cream
salt and white pepper to taste

Garnish: dry sherry, butter,
   oyster crackers

1. Rinse off salt pork rind and pat dry before dicing.

2. Sauté pork over medium-high heat. When about 1 T fat is rendered, remove pork.

3. Sauté onion in pork fat.

4. Add potatoes, clam juice, and water.

5. Boil over medium heat 5 minutes (or until potatoes are nearly done).

6. Add clams and half and half and heat to scalding. Do not boil.

7. Salt and pepper to taste.

8. Ladle enough clams and potatoes into each bowl and add broth. Float a dab of butter atop each. Serve with a bowl of oyster crackers and a cruet of sherry at the table.

If you're the type of person who thought you'd never make a good doctor, don't shuck your own clams. But if you do decide to embark on this awesome adventure, buy the large hardshell cherrystone or quahaug clams. They will probably be prescrubbed. Place them in a 425 degree oven for 10 minutes until they jump, sizzle, and pop open. Drain and reserve all the clam juice. Pry open the shells with fingers and tongs, cutting the muscle that holds the shell together. Scrape out the black stomach contents of each clam and rinse remaining meat under cold water.

This is a chowder that is basic and good. We learned about adding sherry at the house of an English family. A cruet of sherry was passed around and the good taste of the custom stuck. Downeasters might frown, but we doubt they'll ever try to outlaw sherry as they once tried to outlaw Manhattan chowder (made with tomatoes and clams) in Maine.

Apple cider

Anadama

³/₄ C hot reconstituted dry milk
3 T sweet butter
¹/₂ C yellow cornmeal
2 T blackstrap molasses
1¹/₂ t salt
1 T yeast
¹/₄ C warm water

1 egg, slightly beaten
¹/₄ C wheat germ
3 C unbleached all-purpose flour
2 t melted sweet butter
1 T cornmeal
1 t salt

1. In bread bowl pour hot milk over butter, cornmeal, molasses, and salt. Stir to dissolve.

2. Dissolve yeast in water. Add yeast and egg to lukewarm milk mixture.

3. Add wheat germ and 1¹/₂ C flour. Hand beat 1 minute. Add 1¹/₂ C more flour.

4. Knead 5 minutes.

5. Place in oiled loaf pan, cover, and let rise until doubled in bulk (approximately 2 hours).

6. Brush top with melted butter. Sprinkle on 1 T cornmeal mixed with salt.

7. Place in cool oven and bake at 350 degrees for 40 minutes or until golden brown.

Every cookbook in the world tells the story of Anadama, including this one: A listless fishwife habitually neglected to bake bread, so her husband cursed, "Anna, damn her!" and promptly threw this bread together himself.

Unlike some other Anadamas, this recipe should come out with a fine, close-textured loaf. The blackstrap molasses darkens it to a New England maple brown and helps produce a nutritious, sturdy bread. It's easy to prepare, keeps well, and makes a good peanut butter and jam or honey sandwich. Use it also a few days later for French toast with authentic maple syrup over a nugget of melting butter and you have a 3-star breakfast.

Colby cheese

Parsnip–Carrot Soup

Serves 4

2 medium carrots (approximately
    1 C sliced)
2 medium parsnips (approximately
    1 C sliced)
2 C chicken stock
1 T lemon juice

2 C milk
1/8 t nutmeg
salt

Garnish: *thin orange slices*

1. Wash and scrape carrots and parsnips.

2. Slice them into the chicken broth in a small pan. Add lemon juice and cook covered at a slow boil for 45 minutes.

3. Put carrot–parsnip mixture into the blender with 1 C milk. Blend well.

4. Return mixture to pot. Add remaining cup of milk, nutmeg, and salt to taste.

5. Heat. Do not boil.

6. Ladle into bowls and garnish with orange slices.

Parsnips are not our favorite vegetable. However, this soup tames their woody texture and their aggressive taste. With the carrots, they make a mellow blend. If you compliment someone on a pair of socks, he or she isn't well dressed. Otherwise, the socks wouldn't stand out but would blend right into the rest of the attire. This soup is well dressed.

Chablis

Orange Sticky Buns

1 T yeast
1/4 C warm water
4 T sweet butter
3/4 t salt
3 T honey
1 egg, slightly beaten
1 t grated orange rind
1 C hot milk
4 C unbleached all-purpose flour
corn oil

FILLING:

1/4 C sweet butter
3/4 C sugar
grated rind of 1 large
  orange

GLAZE:

1/2 C sugar
1/4 C orange juice
1/4 C light corn syrup
grated rind of 1 orange

1. Dissolve yeast in 1/4 C warm water.

2. Place butter, salt, honey, egg, 1 t orange rind in bread bowl. Pour hot milk into bowl. Stir to melt butter.

3. When milk is warm, add yeast.

4. Add 2 1/2 C flour. Beat 200 strokes.

5. Add 1 1/2 C flour and mix. Dough will be sticky.

6. Brush dough with corn oil. Cover and let rise in same bowl until doubled in bulk (1 1/2–2 hours).

7. Stir down. Place on floured bread board. Knead, adding minimum extra flour to keep from sticking.

8. For filling, cream together butter and sugar. Add rind of 1 large orange.

9. Roll dough into 1/4-inch thick rectangle. Pat filling evenly over dough with fingers.

10. Cut dough in half lengthwise. Roll each half lengthwise and pinch edges together. Place on large baking sheet and chill for approximately 1 hour.

11. Cut 1-inch thick rolls. Place rolls flat side down, close but not touching each other, in oiled cake pans or on large baking sheet. Let rise until nearly doubled in bulk (1 hour).

12. Bake 10–12 minutes at 400 degrees.

13. Make glaze by slowly boiling sugar, orange juice, and corn syrup together in sauce pan for 10 minutes. Stir frequently. Add orange rind.

14. Pour glaze over hot cooked rolls.

All these many steps are necessary for a just dessert. These rolls are light, sweet, sticky, and addictive. If they are baked in cake pans, the leftovers may be wrapped and frozen in the pans ready to be heated for breakfast or tea.

Bonbel cheese

Peanut Butter Soup

Serves 4

²/₃ C smooth peanut butter
   (all natural)
¹/₂ C tomato paste
¹/₃ C mashed ripe banana
5 C chicken stock

¹/₄ C heavy cream
¹/₈ t cayenne (or more to taste)
salt to taste

Garnish: *minced parsley*

1. Place peanut butter, tomato paste, and banana in blender with 2 C of the stock and blend well.

2. Place remaining 3 C stock in a medium-size sauce pan.

3. Heat stock. Add the puréed ingredients and cream.

4. Stir well. Add cayenne and salt to taste.

This one sounds peculiar, we know, but the combination (which is a take-off of an African ground-nut soup) will keep people not only guessing but supping as well. The color is just as appetizing, a cross between a sunset and a peach.

Lager beer

Spinach-Stuffed Rolls

Makes 2 dozen

1 T yeast
1/4 C warm water
1 C water
1 t salt
1 T corn oil
2/3 C graham flour
2 C unbleached all-purpose flour

FILLING:
2 rashers lean bacon
1 lb. fresh spinach
1 medium onion, diced
1 T olive oil
2 t sesame seeds, toasted
1 t lemon juice
salt and pepper to taste

1. Dissolve yeast in warm water.

2. Add 1 C water, salt, oil.

3. Stir in graham and 1 C all-purpose flours. Beat 200 strokes. Add another cup all-purpose flour.

4. Knead 10 minutes, adding small extra amounts of flour as needed to prevent sticking.

5. Cover. Let rise until doubled in bulk (1½ hours).

6. Broil bacon. Cool and break into pieces.

7. Steam spinach. Squeeze out liquid. Chop spinach finely.

8. Sauté onion in oil until soft and transparent.

9. Mix bacon, spinach, onion, and sesame seeds. Add lemon juice. Salt and pepper to taste.

10. Roll out 1/3 dough at a time to less than 1/8 inch thickness. With knife cut 2½ × 2½ inch squares. Place a heaping teaspoon of spinach filling in center. Form (don't roll) into miniature loaves and seal tightly. Tuck ends underneath.

11. Place well apart on lightly oiled baking sheet. Bake 15–20 minutes at 350 degrees or until delicately browned. Remove from oven and brush with butter. Serve hot.

Finger foods offer an added pleasure when the insides contain hidden tastes, as these rolls do. For future use they may be wrapped and frozen immediately after shaping and before they rise. If you do freeze them, brush the tops with melted butter before baking. This will insure that the rolls remain soft in case they dried out during freezing. Good for hors d'oeuvres, too.

Medjools dates

Pimento Soup

Serves 4 small portions

24 whole blanched almonds
4 whole pimentos
2 T olive oil
4 peppercorns
3 cloves garlic, minced
1 t minced parsley
1 t saffron

2 ¹/₂ C boiling water
2 slices French or Italian bread
  (may be a day old) cut into
  1-inch squares

Garnish: French bread fried
  in olive oil, crouton size

1. To blanch almonds drop them in boiling water for 2 minutes and then run cold water over them. Slip off skins by holding almond at the base with thumb and index finger and pressing.

2. Halve the almonds. Dry them on paper towels. Fry them in oil until they are a dark golden color on both sides. Remove with a slotted spoon.

3. Add all the other ingredients to the oil over medium heat. Stir and fry for 5 minutes.

4. In a mortar pound the ingredients with a pestle until they make a fine paste. This may also be done by first passing the ingredients through a sieve or food mill and then mashing them with the back of a wooden spoon into a smooth paste.

5. Put this mixture in a sauce pan and when you're ready to eat pour on the boiling water. Keep on hot burner until ready to serve.

This was originally called almond soup, but the red pepper definitely predominates. As tempting as it might be to use a blender or food processor in this recipe, don't. The soup will turn out tasting like a sandbox special. The essence of the ingredients must be pressed out. This takes sheer muscle, but pumping iron provides startling and delicious results.

Spanish red wine

Saffron Rolls

Makes 14

2 t saffron threads
¹/₄ C water
2 T sweet butter
1 T honey
³/₄ C buttermilk
1 T yeast
1 large egg, slightly beaten
2¹/₂–2³/₄ C unbleached all-
  purpose flour

¹/₂ t salt
¹/₄ t baking soda
1 fresh lemon rind, grated
¹/₄ t allspice
¹/₄ t coriander
¹/₃ C currants

1. Steep saffron threads in ¹/₄ C boiling water for 5 minutes. Reserve both water and threads.

2. Melt butter and honey in heated buttermilk. Cool to warm. Dissolve yeast in buttermilk. After stirring, add saffron threads and water. Cool.

3. Add egg to buttermilk mixture.

4. Mix flour, salt, baking soda, lemon rind, allspice, and coriander.

5. Combine 2 C flour and buttermilk mixtures. Beat well. Add ¹/₄ C flour. Dough will be sticky.

6. On board knead in more flour as needed (approximately ¹/₃ C). Then knead in currants.

7. Place in oiled bowl. Cover and let rise until doubled in bulk (1¹/₂ hours).

8. Punch down. Divide into 14 equal pieces. Round off and place well apart in 2 lightly oiled 8-inch cake pans. Cover. Let rise until doubled in bulk (45 minutes).

9. Bake at 350 degrees for 15–20 minutes or until browned.

Saffron threads are the stamens of the autumn crocus. Their chief virtue lies in the vibrant jonquil color, not their taste. This recipe yields mildly sweet rolls that are soft and butter yellow.

Muenster cheese

Posole

1 large chicken breast
1 lb. loin country-style pork ribs
1 fresh pork hock (unsmoked)
1 beef marrow bone
8 C water
2 T minced onion
2 t salt
2 C prepared **posole** (2 C canned
   whole hominy may be substituted)
2 C whole peeled tomatoes and juice

2 cloves garlic, minced
1 T green jalapeña chili sauce
1 T chili powder
¼ t oregano
salt to taste

Garnish: ½ C chopped onion,
   ½ C chopped green pepper,
   1 C shredded lettuce

1. Soak *posole* overnight. Boil separately in water to cover until kernels explode and puff out like popcorn. This may take 2–3 hours. Add water as needed to keep at same level. Drain and reserve.

2. Place first 7 ingredients in a large soup pot. Bring to a boil. Reduce heat and boil slowly for 3 hours.

3. After 3 hours, remove marrow from beef bone. Cut bite-size pieces of meat from other bones and put these and marrow into the soup. Discard the bones.

4. Add *posole* or hominy, tomatoes, garlic, chili sauce and powder, extra salt to taste, and oregano for ½ hour more cooking time.

5. Serve with small pottery bowls of chopped vegetables on the table.

This cook first had posole *at a small* bodega *in San Miguel de Allende, Mexico. The recipe went something like this: "Take the cracked corn and boil it with a pig's head, hocks, and tomatoes for 3 hours." After a genuine effort (with a few substitutions) this gringo returned with a tale of woe. The corn wouldn't soften. After 3 hours, only a squirrel could eat it. "But you must boil it first in lye, and after that take each kernel and remove the hull."* Posole *was dropped from the repertoire. Then one day we discovered prepared* posole, *cracked corn which has been presoaked and hulled. One New York friend remembers* posole *as samp, a typical Long Island cracked corn dish boiled with salt pork for hours on end. Take our advice. Buy the prepared* posole *or whole canned cooked hominy.*

Mexican beer

Fry Bread

*1¹/₂ C unbleached all-purpose
    flour
1¹/₂ t baking powder
¹/₄ t salt*

*¹/₄ C dry milk
³/₄ C warm water
corn oil, at least 1 C*

1. Mix flour, baking powder, salt, and milk.

2. Add water and mix.

3. Knead a few minutes until smooth. Cover and let rest for 15–20 minutes.

4. Pinch off egg-size pieces and roll less than ¹/₈ inch thin. Take dough in hands and stretch the pieces into irregular shapes, making tissue-thin sections.

5. In 1¹/₂–2-inch deep hot oil (365 degrees), fry on both sides until golden (1 minute or less).

6. Remove. Dab with paper towel. Serve at once.

We first ate these scrumptious breads in a small café in the Navajo country of the New Mexico desert and found them irresistible. They balloon and bubble up into all sorts of playful shapes. As soon as we returned home we experimented and came up with this easy recipe. Like the more refined sopapillas, *fry (or fried) bread is traditionally served with butter and honey. Eat them this way or sprinkle them with confectioners' sugar or a cinnamon–sugar mixture immediately after frying.*

Chihuahua cheese

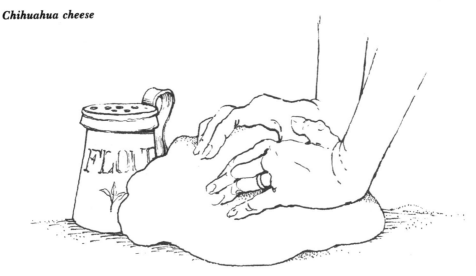

Pumpkin Curry Soup

Serves 4

2 C fresh pumpkin
  (one 2 ¹/₂ lb. pumpkin)
3 T minced onion
2 T sweet butter
3 C chicken stock
1 C grated sharp Cheddar cheese
One 5.3 oz. can evaporated
  milk or ²/₃ C light cream

salt and white pepper
¹/₈ t nutmeg
¹/₂ t curry powder

Garnish: *unpeeled diced apple
  and raisins*

1. Cut pumpkin in half, scoop out seeds (reserve). Place each pumpkin half face down on a baking sheet and bake 30–40 minutes at 350 degrees. (If you are baking gingerbread, the pumpkin may go in the oven with it.)

2. Scoop pumpkin pulp out of baked shells.

3. Sauté onion in butter until soft.

4. In a blender purée 1 C pumpkin with 1 C stock and onion.

5. Repeat with 1 C pumpkin and 1 C stock.

6. With a whisk blend pumpkin, remaining stock, Cheddar cheese, and evaporated milk in heavy sauce pan. Heat and stir to melt cheese.

7. Salt and white pepper to taste.

8. Stir in nutmeg and curry. Serve with bowls of diced apple and raisins on the side.

The pumpkin seeds may be washed, drained, salted, toasted in a slow oven, and served as crunchy hot hors d'oeuvres. For added festivity, cut the top off a 3–4 pound pumpkin. Remove the inside and heat with boiling water (like a teapot) 10 minutes. Drain the pumpkin and fill it with pumpkin curry soup. Serve at the table from the pumpkin tureen.

Apple cider

Gingerbread

2 C sifted cake flour
2 t baking powder
$^1/_2$ t baking soda
$^1/_2$ t salt
2 t ginger
$^1/_4$ t ground cloves
$1^1/_4$ t cinnamon
$^1/_4$ t nutmeg

3 T cocoa
$^1/_2$ C sweet butter
$^1/_2$ C dark brown sugar
1 large egg
$^1/_2$ C blackstrap molasses
$^1/_2$ C honey
$^3/_4$ C buttermilk
$^1/_4$ C milk

1. Mix flour, baking powder, baking soda, salt, ginger, cloves, cinnamon, nutmeg, cocoa. Set aside.

2. Cream butter and brown sugar.

3. Beat egg into butter and sugar until light.

4. Warm molasses and honey, stirring constantly. Remove from heat.

5. Stir buttermilk and milk into molasses and honey.

6. Add the molasses and egg mixtures alternately to flour mixture.

7. Pour into oiled 8 × 8-inch pan. Bake 35–40 minutes at 350 degrees, or until done (the edge should separate from the pan sides and the center should bounce back when lightly pressed).

Perhaps the oldest sweet bread in the world, gingerbread originated among the ancient Egyptians and since then its familiar edgy spice has been a favorite in many forms. This recipe produces a rich, dark, moist cake. Our favorite way to serve it is topped with sliced ripe bananas and mounds of fresh whipped cream, and dusted with coriander.

Waldorf salad

Scallop Soup, St. Jacques

Serves 4

¹/₂ C dry white wine
¹/₂ C water
4 peppercorns
1 bay leaf
1 sprig parsley
2 T minced shallots
1 C chicken broth
³/₄ lb. sea scallops
2 T sweet butter

1 T flour
1 C light cream
¹/₄ C grated Parmesan cheese
¹/₄ C grated Gruyère cheese
1 egg yolk
salt and cayenne to taste

Garnish: *fresh minced parsley*

1. Place wine, water, peppercorns, bay leaf, parsley, shallots, and chicken broth in a sauce pan and bring to a boil.

2. Lower heat and add scallops (cut into bite size). Boil them gently in this liquid for approximately 10 minutes, or until they are tender.

3. Strain the broth into a bowl. Save the scallops and shallots but discard parsley, peppercorns, and bay leaf.

4. Melt butter in a small sauce pan and stir in flour with a whisk. Add light cream and cheese. As soon as this mixture thickens, remove from heat and stir in the scallop broth.

5. Place egg yolk, scallops, shallots, and 2 C of the liquid in a blender or run through a food mill. Purée well.

6. Return all ingredients to a large soup pan and heat. Do not boil.

7. Serve in small portions garnished with minced parsley.

The term St. Jacques used to apply to scallops served in the shell. But since scallops are rarely sold in the shell in this country, the term is indiscriminately applied to any dish that includes scallops, or often the combination of scallops and cheese. This soup rises to any occasion, like Venus on the halfshell.

Muscadet

Buttermilk Yeast Biscuits

Makes 10–12

1 T yeast
2 T warm water
1/2 T honey
1 egg, slightly beaten
2/3 C buttermilk

2 1/4 C unbleached all-purpose
   flour
1/2 t baking soda
1 t salt
3 T sweet butter

1. Dissolve yeast in warm water.

2. Add honey, egg, buttermilk.

3. Mix flour, soda, and salt in separate bowl.

4. Cut butter into flour to make cornmeal-like texture.

5. Combine buttermilk and flour mixtures.

6. Pat together on board (don't knead). Roll very lightly to 1/2-inch thickness. Shape with biscuit cutter or small drinking glass. Place loosely in buttered cake pans.

7. Let rise 1/2 hour or more until doubled in bulk.

8. Bake 10 minutes at 425 degrees or until golden.

Served straight from the oven, these are petal light with a rich buttermilk flavor. You may brush the tops with milk before baking to darken them. This recipe takes a little more time than standard baking powder biscuits, but the result is much lighter. In larger shapes, these biscuits are also delicious sliced in half and covered with fresh sweetened strawberries and fresh whipped cream.

Gruyère cheese

Scotch Broth

Serves 4–6

1 1/2 lbs. lamb shoulder with
    bone in, cut into 2-inch pieces
10 C water
salt
1/2 C diced carrot
1/2 C diced celery

1 C chopped leeks
3 T pearl barley
freshly ground black pepper

Garnish: *mint sprigs*

1. Place lamb in the soup pot with water.

2. Bring to a boil and turn heat to medium-low. Cook at slow boil covered for 1 hour. Salt broth to taste.

3. Remove lamb. Pour broth into a bowl and skim off excess fat. Wash any black scum from the soup pot and return lamb and broth to pot.

4. Add vegetables. Bring to boil and reduce heat.

5. Cook at slow boil another hour, adding barley during the last half hour of cooking.

6. Remove the meat and bones with a slotted spoon.

7. Pepper to taste.

8. Remove lamb from the bones and cut into small pieces. Add to the soup.

9. Serve in pottery bowls.

This is a stalwart soup. The essentials are the barley and lamb. Scotch broth was a standard while this cook was growing up, a family hand-me-down from the bonny industrial hills of Dunkirk, Scotland.

Stout

Scones

1 C graham flour
1/2 t cream of tartar
1 t baking soda

1/4 t salt
1/4 C sweet butter
1/3 C light cream

1. Mix flour, cream of tartar, baking soda, and salt.

2. Cut in butter.

3. Stir in cream.

4. Pat gently (do not roll) into circular mound that is 1/2 inch thick at edge and 1 1/2–2 inches at center.

5. Cut into 4 equal triangular pieces. Place apart on lightly oiled baking sheet. Brush with cream.

6. Bake at 400 degrees for 15 minutes or until browned on top.

These scones come closer to what the Scots had in mind than the latter-day version, which merely resembles another kind of American baking powder biscuit. This simple, quick-to-make recipe produces grainy, nutty-tasting scones. They're full bodied and crumbly and offer a refreshing change of texture. Stone-ground whole wheat may be substituted for the coarse graham flour—the coarser the better.

Honey

Senegalese Soup

2 T sweet butter
1 1/2 T flour
2 t curry
3 C chicken stock
2 egg yolks
1/2 C half and half

1/3 C yogurt
1 C shredded cooked chicken meat
salt to taste

Garnish: *diced tart apple*

1. Melt butter in a large sauce pan and stir in flour and curry.

2. Add chicken stock and bring to a boil over medium-high heat. Remove from flame.

3. In separate bowl, whip yolks, half and half, and yogurt.

4. Pour this mixture in a thin stream into the curry stock, stirring constantly.

5. Remove the chicken from the bones and cut or shred into tiny pieces. Add chicken to soup. Salt to taste.

6. Return soup to heat and simmer (but do not boil) for 15 minutes or until it thickens.

7. Serve hot or ice cold.

Curry is a condiment composed of 10 to 16 spices. The base for curry powder is the golden turmeric pod. More curry may be added to taste. Served cold, the natural gelatin in the chicken stock may gel in the refrigerator. If it does, beat in a bit of half and half until the soup is the desired consistency.

Ceylon black tea

Puris

1 C unbleached all-purpose flour
1 C graham flour
$^1/_2$ t salt
2 T corn oil

1 T honey
$^3/_4$ C yogurt
$^1/_4$ C tahini
corn oil (at least 1 C)

1. Mix flours and salt.

2. Stir together oil, honey, yogurt, and tahini.

3. Combine flours and liquids.

4. Knead 5 minutes. Dough will be stiff.

5. Cover the dough and let sit 1 hour at room temperature.

6. Pinch off small fist-size pieces and roll $^1/_8$ inch thin. Place 5-inch diameter bowl on dough and cut out circles.

7. Deep fry individually in hot oil (365 degrees) until puffed and lightly toasted on both sides (less than 1 minute). Drain on paper towels. Serve warm.

This variation of East Indian puris *has a nutty flavor. The circles, which puff into balloon-like shells, are intriguing to cook and unusual to serve and eat. What's more, they're simple to prepare. A wok makes an excellent deep fryer for these. Put enough oil in the wok so that the* puris *will float and have enough room to expand. The tahini (ground sesame seeds) supplements the "wheaty" taste of the graham flour and adds more nutrients. You may keep them warm longer in an aluminum-lined, cloth-covered bread basket.*

Honeybutter

Sorrel Soup

Serves 4

3/4 lb. sorrel
1/2 C diced onion
1/4 C sweet butter
1 C light cream or
    half and half

1 egg yolk (large egg),
    slightly beaten
3 C chicken stock
salt and white pepper

Garnish: *freshly grated nutmeg*

1. De-stem, rinse, and drain sorrel leaves.

2. Stack the sorrel leaves. Then slice thin strips off layered leaves.

3. Sauté onion in butter until golden and soft. Add sorrel strips and simmer covered until wilted (approximately 5 minutes).

4. In separate bowl beat together egg yolk with cream or half and half.

5. Boil stock. Remove stock from heat and slowly add yolk mixture while stirring with wire whisk.

6. Return pot to low heat. Do not boil.

7. Add sorrel–onion mixture. Season soup with salt and white pepper.

8. Grate nutmeg on top of each serving.

Sorrel looks like a spinach leaf and tastes like lemon because of its high acid content. Several different sorrels grow in the wild: Those with the botanical name Rumex *(dock and its relatives), wood sorrels, and mountain sorrel, which is a member of the buckwheat family and is gathered by Eskimo and Indian tribes. Although these wild sorrels are edible, the French and broadleaf varieties are much more appetizing and abundant when cultivated. This soup is known as* Potage Germiny *by the French. It is the* pièce de résistance *for a light special luncheon.*

Folle Blanche

110

Whole Wheat Bread

Makes 2 loaves

2 T yeast
1/2 C warm water
1 T salt
2 T corn oil
1 large egg, slightly beaten

1 1/2 C lukewarm water
2 C graham flour
1/4 C bran flakes
3 1/2 C unbleached all-purpose
   flour

1. In bread bowl dissolve yeast in 1/2 C warm water.

2. Stir in salt, oil, egg.

3. Add 1 1/2 C lukewarm water.

4. Mix in graham flour, bran flakes, and 1 C all-purpose flour. Beat 5 minutes.

5. Stir in 2 C all-purpose flour. Mix in with fingers.

6. Knead on bread board 10 minutes, adding extra flour (up to 1/2 C) as needed to prevent sticking.

7. Place dough in oiled bowl, cover, and let rise until doubled in bulk (2 hours).

8. Punch down. Divide in half. Round off into 2 loaves. Place in oiled bread pans. Let rise to tops of pans (1 hour).

9. Brush tops with water. Bake at 400 degrees for 25–30 minutes or until done. Remove from pans and cool on wire rack. Brush tops with butter while loaves are still warm.

A second rising and proofing will make a lighter loaf, but it's not necessary, especially if you're short on time. The egg adds a velvety texture, longer storage time, and more nutrients. A heavier, darker, denser loaf may be made by using less all-purpose flour and more graham. The exact amount of flour must be up to you. Depending on how much moisture is in the air and the flour, you could use even less flour than suggested here. The loaves will be varnished with a mahogany-colored crust and have a robust brown taste.

Tybo cheese

Spinach–Celery Soup

Serves 6

¹/₂ lb. fresh spinach
1 C diced celery
2 T minced shallots
1 C chicken stock
¹/₂ C spinach liquid
2 T sweet butter
1 T flour

2¹/₂ C milk
¹/₂ t tarragon
salt and white pepper to taste
2 T grated Parmesan cheese

Garnish: *crisp bacon bits*

1. Wash spinach thoroughly and de-stem. Drain.

2. Remove tough outer fibers of celery stalks and dice.

3. Add celery and shallots to chicken stock. Cover and boil slowly for 10 minutes.

4. At the same time boil down the spinach, covered (no water) over medium-low heat. A half pound yields approximately 1 C.

5. Drain and press the spinach in a strainer, reserving liquid.

6. Finely chop the spinach.

7. Over medium heat melt butter. Add flour, stirring with a whisk. Slowly add milk and cook stirring for 5 minutes.

8. Add celery and stock mixture, spinach and spinach liquid, tarragon, salt and white pepper to taste.

9. Heat to near boiling and whip in Parmesan.

Spinach–celery soup is a perfect light luncheon dish. It's also a good soup to rouse the appetite, tasty but not too heavy, and high in iron.

Pinot chardonnay

Cream Rolls

3/4 T yeast
3 T warm water
1/2 t salt (scant)

1 large egg, slightly beaten
1 C heavy cream
2 C unbleached all-purpose flour

1. Dissolve yeast in water. Add salt.

2. Stir together egg and cream. Combine with yeast mixture.

3. Add 1 C flour. Beat 100 strokes. Add 1 C more flour and mix.

4. On board knead lightly for 30 seconds. Add minimum amount of flour to prevent sticking.

5. Shape into round rolls 2 inches in diameter. Place in buttered cake pans. Let rise until doubled in bulk (1½–2 hours).

6. Brush with cream or milk. Bake 15–20 minutes (depending on size) at 400 degrees.

These are porous, light, spongy rolls. The subtle cream taste creates a velvety texture not found in hard-shortening rolls and biscuits. While they are hot, spread them with sweet butter and homemade red raspberry jam. If past is prologue, people who normally eat one or two rolls at a meal will devour three or four of these.

Edam cheese

Szechwan Soup

Serves 4

1/3 C pork, fish, or chicken
  (shredded if cooked, or
  sliced if raw)
1 T dry sherry
1 T corn starch
1/8 C wood ears
1/8 C golden needles
  (dried day-lily buds)
2 T corn starch
1/2 C water
2 T chopped scallions

1 C vegetable of choice (pea pods,
  celery, bok choy, cabbage,
  spinach)
2 T peanut oil
3 1/2 C chicken stock
soy sauce to taste
2 T vinegar
1/4 t Chinese hot sauce or
  Tabasco

Garnish: 1/2 C bean curd, cubed

1. Raw fish, pork, or chicken may be used, or leftovers. Slice the raw ingredients in fine 1-inch strips or shred cooked ingredients. Marinate meat, fowl, or fish in sherry mixed with 1 T corn starch while preparing vegetables.

2. Soak wood ears and golden needles in boiling water for 15 minutes. Snap off any hard pieces from wood ears and hard stems from needles. Squeeze water from both. Cut needles in half and slice wood ears into thin 1-inch-long pieces.

3. Mix 2 T corn starch with 1/2 C water.

4. Chop scallions and slice vegetables into thin diagonal 1–2-inch strips.

5. Coat bottom of wok or heavy frying pan with peanut oil and heat. Add pork, fish, or chicken to oil with scallions.

6. Stir fry for 2 minutes. Add the vegetables and stir fry another 2 minutes. If frozen vegetable is used, cook under steamer cover. Add 1/2 C corn starch water.

7. Add the chicken stock and soy sauce to taste. Mix vinegar and hot sauce in large serving bowl which has been preheated with hot water.

8. Pour soup into vinegar mixture. Szechwan soup is ladled into rice bowls at the table. Diners may help themselves to bean curd.

This soup requires little cooking time if the stock is already prepared. About 20 minutes are spent preparing meats and vegetables, stir frying and boiling.

We prefer raw pork chops and snow peas, but a variety of ingredients may be substituted, including the chicken used to make the stock. Golden needles, wood ears, dark soy sauce, bean curd, and Chinese hot sauce may all be purchased at Chinese shops and in some health food stores. A word of caution: If the chicken stock is heavily salted, not as much soy sauce is needed in the soup. So if you make the stock, don't salt it.

Jasmine tea

Egg Rolls

ROLL:
1 scant C unbleached all-
  purpose flour
1/4 t salt
1/3 C water

FILLING:
1 T peanut oil
1 C diced celery
2 scallions, diced
1 clove garlic, minced
1/8 t grated ginger root

2/3 C diced water chestnuts
3 diced mushrooms
1/2 C mung bean sprouts
1/2 C alfalfa sprouts
1/8 t sugar
1 T soy sauce (or more to taste)
1 egg, slightly beaten
peanut oil for deep frying

1. Mix flour and salt. Stir in water.

2. Knead 5–10 minutes until smooth and elastic. Cover and set aside for 1/2 hour.

3. Prepare vegetables.

4. Heat wok (or iron frying pan) and add 1 T oil. When hot, stir fry celery, scallions, and garlic only a few minutes until celery is slightly transparent yet crisp.

5. Grate ginger root directly into wok. Add chestnuts, mushrooms, sprouts, sugar, and soy sauce. Mix all together and stir fry 2 minutes. Cool.

6. Roll dough into very thin 15 × 15-inch square. This requires rolling, turning dough over, and rolling on the other side. Repeat this a half dozen times or so until the right size is reached.

7. Measure with ruler to get exact square, trimming off excess dough. Cut into nine 5-inch squares.

8. Place heaping tablespoon of filling diagonally across center of square. Make tight compact packages: 1) Fold bottom triangular point over filling; 2) fold both side points over to center of filling and brush seams with egg to seal; 3) fold top point over filling, completely enclosing contents. Brush with egg to seal.

9. When all rolls are formed, deep fry in hot peanut oil (380 degrees) until crisp and richly golden. Place on absorbent paper. Serve hot.

The dough for these egg rolls is worked somewhat like strudel dough–stretching it, rolling, turning, and rolling more. Many variations on the filling may be made, including those using cooked ground pork and seafood cut into small pieces with Chinese vegetables.

Fresh pineapple chunks

Tomato Soup

Serves 4

6–8 medium tomatoes, quartered
2½ C chicken stock
½ t basil
½ t thyme
¼ t oregano (imported is less
   bitter)
salt and freshly ground white pepper

4 T tomato paste
½ C cream, yogurt, or sour
   cream

Garnish: minced fresh basil
   or dill

1. Slowly boil tomatoes in chicken stock with herbs for 15 minutes.

2. Run mixture through a sieve or fine disc of food mill and pour purée back into pot.

3. Salt and pepper to taste.

4. Stir in tomato paste. (If soup is not of the desired consistency, boil an extra 10 minutes or add more paste.)

5. Add ½ C cream. (Yogurt or sour cream add a different flavor to the soup.)

6. Heat slowly. Do not boil.

7. Serve in bowls that offset the bright red.

Basic. Easy. Good. Garden fresh tomatoes and herbs in season, of course, are best. Using imagination will rarely spoil this soup. Try dill or sorrel as a substitute. Add a little dry wine if you have some on hand. Double or triple the recipe and freeze as a base for other soups and sauces. If you're on a diet, yogurt is a good substitute for cream.

Pilsner beer

Cheese Biscuits

1 C unbleached all-purpose flour
1/4 t salt
1 1/2 t baking powder
dash of paprika

2 1/2 T sweet butter
1/2 C shredded sharp Cheddar
   cheese
1 t prepared mustard
1/3 C milk

1. Mix flour, salt, baking powder, paprika.

2. Cut in butter.

3. Mix in cheese.

4. Stir mustard into milk.

5. With a fork gradually stir the milk into flour mixture.

6. Gently press dough together several times. Do not knead.

7. Gently roll out to 1/2-inch thickness.

8. With biscuit cutter or 2 1/2-inch diameter drinking glass cut circles in dough. Place biscuits nearly touching each other in 8-inch ungreased cake pan. Brush tops with milk.

9. Bake 10–12 minutes at 450 degrees.

Baking powder biscuits have strong roots in the pioneering West but they needn't be hard as a horseshoe. Two guarantees: First, stir and handle the dough too much and you'll bake hard biscuits; second, work slowly, carefully, and with a light touch and you'll end up with flaky biscuits that break apart with a look. Rather than using a rolling pin, gently work the dough into one flat 1/2-inch thick layer for cutting. Take a few extra seconds to do this. It's worth it.

Cheddar cheese

Vegetable–Short Rib Soup

Serves 6–8

5 C water
1/2 C diced onion
1 bay leaf
1 T minced fresh celery leaves
2 lbs. short ribs, cut into
  3-inch pieces
1/4 C barley
3/4 C diced potato

3/4 C diced carrot
3/4 C diced celery
1 C chopped cabbage
1 C fresh whole peeled tomatoes
salt and freshly ground black
  pepper to taste

Garnish: *minced chives*

1. Bring water, onion, bay leaf, and celery leaves to a boil in wide-bottomed soup pot.

2. Add short ribs. Lower heat and boil slowly 1 1/2 hours.

3. Remove meat.

4. The meat will leave a fat layer floating on top. Degrease the soup with a large spoon.

5. Add barley to soup and cook covered at slow boil 1/2 hour.

6. Add vegetables, salt and pepper. Cover, and boil slowly 20 minutes.

7. Place meat in shallow baking dish and put it in the oven to crisp and brown at 350 degrees while vegetables cook.

8. Serve short ribs in separate dish at the table.

Vegetable soup is universal. This is a family recipe and changes with the season, the generation, and the mood of the cook. Any vegetable on hand may be added, although it should be fresh because leftover vegetables tend to get mushy.

Cold milk

Wheat Germ Crackers

1 1/2 C unbleached all-purpose
* flour*
1/4 C toasted wheat germ
1/2 t baking soda
1/2 t salt

2 T corn oil
1 C buttermilk
1 T sesame seeds

1. Mix flour, wheat germ, soda, salt.

2. Stir together oil and buttermilk. Mix thoroughly into flour mixture.

3. Place on lightly oiled 12 × 18-inch baking sheet and press with fingers until dough covers sheet to uniform thickness, about 1/8 inch or thinner if possible. Sprinkle top with flour if sticky.

4. Sprinkle sesame seeds evenly over dough.

5. Press seeds hard into dough with a rolling pin or the palm of your hand.

6. Score dough with knife into 2 × 3-inch rectangles. Puncture tops with fork.

7. Bake 10 minutes at 350 degrees or until golden. Remove from sheet and cool on wire rack.

Be sure to pat the dough into a very thin layer. If you have excess dough, spread on another sheet. Otherwise, the crackers will be thick and chewy. They're better, too, if they're cooked to an obvious crispness to give them a snappy taste and texture.

Aged Cheddar cheese

Watercress Soup (Cold)

Serves 4

2 ¹/₂ C watercress leaves
3 C chicken stock
¹/₃ C sour cream

salt to taste

Garnish: *small rose petals*

1. Remove leaves from watercress stems. Wash and drain. Measure a moderately packed 2¹/₂ C leaves.

2. Make sure to skim fat off chicken stock. Place 2 C of stock in blender with fresh cress and purée well.

3. Add cress liquid to remaining 1 C stock.

4. Salt to taste.

5. Chill thoroughly and serve in chilled wine glasses or water goblets.

Watercress grows wild in brooks and freshets in many states. A childhood pastime was to "go fetch watercress" for the dinner salad in a haunt alive with this water-born peppery plant. If you live too far north for this activity, watercress is still available in small choice stores. Thank goodness there is no such thing as canned, frozen, or freeze-dried cress. It has to be fresh to give that perky, sensationally uplifting taste on a summer's day. Use any leftover cress for bread–butter–watercress canapés.

Earl Grey tea

English Muffins

1 C water
1/3 C dry milk
3/4 t salt
1 t honey
2 T sweet butter

1 T yeast
2 1/2 C unbleached all-purpose
    flour
fine yellow cornmeal

1. In sauce pan mix water, milk, salt, honey, and butter. Heat to dissolve honey and butter. Cool to warm.

2. Dissolve yeast in warm milk mixture.

3. Add 1 3/4 C flour. Beat well.

4. Cover. Let rise until doubled in bulk (1 hour).

5. Stir in 3/4 C flour. Cover and refrigerate 20 minutes.

6. Knead quickly about a minute. Add small amounts of flour to prevent sticking.

7. Roll dough 1/3 inch thick onto greased baking sheet sprinkled with cornmeal.

8. Cut 4-inch circles. Peel away excess dough and leave rounds to rise until nearly tripled in bulk (1/2–1 hour).

9. Cook each side of rounds 5–10 minutes on ungreased griddle over low heat until browned and firm to touch on sides. Cool.

10. With tines of 2 forks back to back, gently divide muffins in half. Toast, butter generously, and serve.

English muffins should be toasted and heaped with butter for their full effect. This home-baked version has a memorable fresh taste. Muffin rings to contain the rounds are available but unnecessary. We've used tuna cans with both ends cut out (a standard method), and find them cumbersome and too small. The muffins hold their shape without molds. Squash them gently with a spatula as they're cooking if they rise too much. Otherwise, the inside will not cook before the outside is browned.

Red raspberry jam

White Onion Wine Soup

3 T sweet butter
1 lb. white onions (approximately 2 heaping C diced onions)
3 C chicken stock
1 1/2 C dry light white wine
  (such as a Folle Blanche)

1/2 lb. grated Cantal cheese
salt and white pepper to taste

Garnish: fresh parsley sprigs

1. Sauté onions in butter. Cover and let simmer over low heat approximately 10 minutes or until soft, stirring occasionally.

2. Whirl onions in blender just 1 second with 1 C chicken stock (or press through coarse disc of food mill).

3. Return onions to soup pot with remaining chicken stock.

4. Boil slowly 10 minutes, covered.

5. Add wine. Boil slowly 5 minutes, uncovered. (The alcohol content of the wine should not be apparent. If it is, heat until it is evaporated.)

6. Slowly stir in the grated cheese, over low heat, until it is completely melted.

7. Add salt and white pepper to taste. (Cheese has salt, so taste the soup first.)

8. This soup may be served with croutons if hard rolls do not accompany the meal.

We have made this soup with a combination of Gruyère mixed with a strong Tilsit when Cantal cheese was unavailable. However, after the cheese is melted, the soup must be served at once before the cheese reverts to its basic texture. This recipe originally called for an expensive Pouilly-Fuissé white Burgundy. The Burgundy seemed too heady for the soup and we were more than heady before we'd finished the first course. A lighter wine like a Folle Blanche has a more delicate taste and is quite a bit cheaper than Pouilly-Fuissé.

Folle Blanche

Hard Rolls

1 T yeast
½ C warm water
1 t salt

¾ C water
2¾–3 C unbleached
   all-purpose flour
fine yellow cornmeal

1. Dissolve yeast in ½ C warm water.

2. Add salt, ¾ C water, and 2 C flour. Stir well. Beat 2–3 minutes.

3. Add ¾ C flour. Knead 10–15 minutes, adding only enough flour to keep from sticking.

4. Cover. Let rise until doubled in bulk (2 hours).

5. Punch down. Divide into 10 equal pieces. Shape into miniature loaves. Place on oiled baking sheet sprinkled with cornmeal. Cover and let rise 1 hour.

6. With razor blade make a ½-inch deep cut the length of each roll. Place large shallow pan containing boiling water on bottom shelf of oven. Bake 20–25 minutes at 350 degrees.

Classic French bread is made from yeast, flour, salt, and water. These rolls use the same basic ingredients and produce a hard stiff roll good for tearing apart and strengthening your teeth. Since no oil or honey is included, these do not keep for long.

Seedless grapes

Yellow Split Pea and Hominy Soup

Serves 4–6

1 1/2 C yellow split peas
7–9 C cold water
1 smoked ham hock
1 T minced fresh celery leaves
1/2 C diced onion
1/2 t thyme

salt and white pepper to taste
one 14–16 oz. can of whole
  hominy (white or yellow)

Garnish: *chopped fresh celery leaves*

1. Wash and drain peas. In large kettle combine with 7 C water, ham hock, celery leaves, and onion.

2. Bring to boil. Reduce heat and boil slowly 1 hour or until thick.

3. If too thick, add water to desired consistency.

4. Season with thyme. Salt and pepper to taste. (The ham hock will be salty, so taste the soup first.)

5. Drain and rinse hominy and add it last. Heat soup to serve.

6. If the meat on the ham hock is good, cut off pieces into each bowl and ladle thick hot pease porridge over the ham.

7. Sprinkle with celery leaves.

This porridge is so sturdy you and your guests will be full for two days. A popular meal when everyone comes in famished after a day of cross-country skiing or snowshoeing. Hominy is whole kernel corn with the hulls removed. It comes in white and yellow and is canned in salt and water. Avoid the mistake of buying hominy grits, which are ground corn and would transform this soup into unstirrable mortar.

Lager beer

Apricot Loaf

Makes 1 loaf

1 C dried apricots
2 C water
1/2 C finely chopped walnuts
1 1/2 C unbleached all-purpose
  flour
1 1/2 C whole wheat flour

1/2 t salt
1 1/4 t baking soda
1/4 C sweet butter
1/2 C dark brown sugar
1/2 C cottage cheese
1 large egg, beaten well
1 C buttermilk

1. In sauce pan boil apricots in 2 C water until soft.

2. Mix walnuts, both flours, salt, and baking soda.

3. In separate bowl cream butter and brown sugar together. Add cottage cheese.

4. Beat egg until light and airy. Fold it into butter–sugar–cottage cheese mixture.

5. Drain apricots, reserving 1/4 C liquid. Mix apricots and juice into butter mixture.

6. Stir buttermilk and butter mixture alternately into flour mixture.

7. Pour batter into oiled bread pan. Bake at 350 degrees for approximately 70 minutes or until paring knife comes out clean from center of loaf. Remove from pan and cool on wire rack.

This is a heavy, moist, dark bread. It is also nutritious and filling. Be careful near the end of the baking, however. Not much leeway is left between cooking the inside and burning the outside. (Cover top with foil if loaf begins to burn before it is done.) This bread keeps well. With cream cheese it is ambrosial. Pop a slice of apricot loaf into your toaster the next morning, too.

Cream cheese

Index